TECHNICAL REPORT

Mitigating Corruption in Government Security Forces

The Role of Institutions, Incentives, and Personnel Management in Mexico

Beth J. Asch • Nicholas Burger • Mary Manqing Fu

RAND INVESTMENT IN PEOPLE AND IDEAS

This report is a product of the RAND Corporation's continuing program of self-initiated independent research. Support for such research is provided, in part, by donors and by the independent research and development provisions of RAND's contracts for the operation of its U.S. Department of Defense federally funded research and development centers. The research was conducted jointly within the RAND National Security Research Division and RAND Infrastructure, Safety, and Environment.

Library of Congress Cataloging-in-Publication Data

Asch, Beth J.
  Mitigating corruption in government security forces : the role of institutions, incentives, and personnel management in Mexico / Beth J. Asch, Nicholas Burger, Mary Manqing Fu.
     p. cm.
  Includes bibliographical references.
  ISBN 978-0-8330-5258-2 (pbk. : alk. paper)
  1. Police—Mexico—Personnel management. 2. Police administration—Mexico. 3. Police corruption—Mexico.
  4. Police—Government policy—Mexico. I. Burger, Nicholas. II. Fu, Mary Manqing. III. Title..

  HV8160.A3A82 2011
  363.2'2—dc23

                                                                            2011033844

The RAND Corporation is a nonprofit institution that helps improve policy and decisionmaking through research and analysis. RAND's publications do not necessarily reflect the opinions of its research clients and sponsors.

RAND® is a registered trademark.

Published 2011 by the RAND Corporation
1776 Main Street, P.O. Box 2138, Santa Monica, CA 90407-2138
1200 South Hayes Street, Arlington, VA 22202-5050
4570 Fifth Avenue, Suite 600, Pittsburgh, PA 15213-2665
RAND URL: http://www.rand.org/
To order RAND documents or to obtain additional information, contact
Distribution Services: Telephone: (310) 451-7002;
Fax: (310) 451-6915; Email: order@rand.org

Preface

Corruption in the Mexican police forces is widely acknowledged and longstanding. The Mexican government has undertaken police reforms in recent years that have focused on professionalizing the Mexican police. Key components of these reforms have been changes in compensation and personnel policies as a way of creating a civil service for police personnel. Whether these reforms are the right ones or have helped are open questions.

In this report, we draw on the literature on corruption and personnel incentives and analyze household survey data and other information related to police reform in Mexico. The study's objectives were to address questions about the roots of corruption and the tools that could be used to mitigate corruption, with a focus on compensation and personnel management policies. We also provide an initial assessment, based on available information, about the effectiveness of these policies. The report should be of interest to the broad policy and research communities concerned about police corruption in general and in Mexico specifically.

This report is a product of the RAND Corporation's continuing program of self-initiated independent research. Support for such research is provided, in part, by donors and by the independent research and development provisions of RAND's contracts for the operation of its U.S. Department of Defense federally funded research and development centers. The research was conducted jointly within the RAND National Security Research Division (NSRD) and RAND Infrastructure, Safety, and Environment (ISE).

NSRD conducts research and analysis on defense and national security topics for the U.S. and allied defense, foreign policy, homeland security, and intelligence communities and foundations and other nongovernmental organizations that support defense and national security analysis.

For more information on the RAND National Security Research Division, see http://www.rand.org/nsrd.html or contact the director (contact information is provided on the web page).

The mission of ISE is to improve the development, operation, use, and protection of society's essential physical assets and natural resources and to enhance the related social assets of safety and security of individuals in transit and in their workplaces and communities.

For more information on ISE, see http://www.rand.org/ise.html or contact the director (contact information is provided on the web page).

Questions or comments about this report are welcome and can be addressed to Beth Asch (Beth_Asch@rand.org) or Nicholas Burger (Nicholas_Burger@rand.org).

Contents

Figures

Tables

Summary

Corruption has been and continues to be a significant challenge for Mexico. There is a widespread belief that many government institutions—perhaps none more than Mexico's police—suffer from corruption, bribery, and a lack of accountability. At more than 400,000 officers across federal, state, and local levels, the police in Mexico play a critical role in enforcing laws, safeguarding the public, and maintaining order, but corruption, favoritism, nepotism, and a lack of professionalism serve to undermine these functions. Moreover, a growing problem with drug cartel activities and narcotics trafficking serves to exacerbate corruption and undermines police accountability, even as the drug trade makes the need for effective law enforcement more acute.

Drug trafficking—and the violence it engenders—has become so severe that the government has turned to the other major component of Mexico's security forces—the military—to provide law and order. Although the public perceives that the police forces are among the most corrupt of Mexican institutions, the military does not share this dubious distinction. Compared with the federal, state, and local police, the military is viewed as more trustworthy and less corrupt. Nevertheless, there are concerns that the increasingly close relationship between the police and military and the role the military is being asked to play in countering cartel activity will expand opportunities for corrupt behavior.

Recent administrations, from the federal government to local municipalities, have attempted various types of police reforms, all in an effort to promote professionalism. These have included national financial support programs targeted at high-crime municipalities, more stringent qualification requirements for new recruits, improved training and technology for officers, and higher salaries. Anecdotally, success has been mixed, and there has been little rigorous assessment either of the factors that most contribute to police corruption or of the reform policies to date. This report assesses the problem of corruption in the Mexican police and security forces—and the options for police reform—through the lens of economics and incentives.

Approach

The goals for the report are two-fold. First, there is a significant literature on the role of economic incentives in promoting an effective labor force and a developing literature on the causes and consequences of corruption; we aim to bring these literatures to bear on Mexico's efforts at police reform. Second, to the extent possible, we want to assess the problem of corruption in the Mexican police through quantitative data and methods.

We begin by reviewing the causes of government corruption and the lessons we can draw from the literature on personnel management and anticorruption. Although little research has specifically addressed efforts to reduce police corruption, the literature as a whole provides insight into the types of policies that are consistent with improving professionalism. Next, we review past and current reforms in Mexico and draw parallels to the economic incentives literature in characterizing Mexico's policies to promote police professionalism.

We then use empirical data to describe households' perceptions and experiences with corruption in Mexico, especially regarding the police and military. We present results from specialized, large-scale household surveys on corruption and crime that cover all 31 states and the federal district at various points over the past decade. These data allow us to assess household views of and experiences with the military and the police, both across states and over time. Although there are not sufficient public data to rigorously evaluate current reforms, we draw on household survey data to assess the indirect effects associated with reforms. Using surveys of income and occupation, we examine key inputs, including education and salaries, that theory predicts will drive police professionalism and affect corruption.

Caveats

We note three important potential limitations of our work. First, we take an economic perspective. Because this perspective has not been dominant in the existing literature on corruption in Mexico, it might offer new insights. On the other hand, our analysis does not always capture the depth of institutional knowledge about Mexican police reform demonstrated by research from other disciplines. Second, where we can, we incorporate quantitative data analysis. Nonetheless, because we do not have access to key administrative data, much of the analysis should be interpreted with caution—as we explain in more detail in Chapter Four. Finally, our analysis focuses on small-scale corruption, such as petty bribery. Although we recognize that Mexico's severe and growing problem with drug-related crime has important implications for corruption, a thorough analysis of the relationship between corruption and drug-related crime is beyond the scope of this report.

Results

The literature review on economic incentives in promoting an effective workforce highlights the importance of weak institutions, a term used in the development literature to refer to such country attributes as the lack of property rights and free markets, as determinants of corruption. Economic institutions are stronger when there are constraints on those who hold power, when power is shared by a broad base of people and institutions, and when there are fewer economic rents to extract, such as those that arise from drug money, from private organizations. Incentive mechanisms can play an important role in promoting workforce management only if leaders and those who define these incentives act in the public interest and are not corrupt. In this case, various mechanisms can improve performance, including promotion systems, pay growth over the career, pay for performance, screening mechanisms, and bonuses. The experience of the U.S. military provides ample evidence of the effectiveness of these mechanisms in the public sector. In the context of corruption, the literature highlights the role of higher pay and dismissal for corrupt employees, though there is only some empirical evidence to support this overall approach.

There is a long history of police reform in Mexico. Previous reforms have been designed to reduce corruption and improve police professionalism, but they have often been uncoordinated across jurisdictions and administrations. At the federal level, there have been multiple, significant reorganizations, either to create new police forces or to combine existing ones. But there is little continuity in reforms across political administrations, something that is true of municipal and state policies as well. More recent federal programs, including the Public Security Support Fund (Fondo de Apoyos para la Seguridad Pública, or FASP) and the Subsidy for Municipal Public Security (Subsidio para la Seguridad Pública Municipal, or SUBSEMUN), are designed to provide structured, targeted financial support for state and municipal police forces. Although it is too early to tell whether these programs are effective, they represent a more coherent effort at achieving an evidence-based approach to improving professionalism.

We find that the police are perceived as highly corrupt, a result that is relatively stable over time and consistent with widespread beliefs about Mexico's police. In contrast, the military are rated the least corrupt government institution, and nearly as low a rating as the church's. However, national trends in corruption perceptions mask more subtle results. Household experiences with corruption are not highly correlated with perceptions: People who are in states where bribes are paid more frequently are not in states with a higher perception of corruption. Moreover, although overall bribery rates have increased between 2001 and 2007, rates of bribes paid for services associated with the police and to most types of police (e.g., state, federal) have remained stable. Relative to overall corruption in terms of bribes paid to any public servant, police corruption appears to have declined.

Due to data limitations and the way reforms have been implemented, we are unable to assess empirically whether past reforms have been effective at reducing corruption. There are few publicly available administrative data on key variables of interest, including police wages, pensions, or other long-term benefits. We lack specific data on key features of past reforms, such as when and how they were implemented; moreover, reforms were often initiated by new administrations or in response to major events, making it difficult to disentangle the effects of reforms from other policy and economic changes.

Instead, we focus on the available microdata on key inputs that the theoretical literature says should affect police professionalization and performance, and we find potentially encouraging evidence of progress. Data from 2000 indicate that, relative to a comparable general population, police and other security-sector workers have lower educational attainment and receive less compensation over the course of their careers. In particular, older officers, who should earn higher wages based on experience, actually earn the same as or less than new recruits. In 2000, fewer police officers had high school diplomas than did nonpolice personnel. For 2008, however, educational attainment is higher for police than the general population, and wages increase across all age cohorts. According to cross-sectional data, average wages across age groups remain relatively flat compared with those of non–security-worker populations; older officers continue to have relatively low salaries.

In summary, the results are suggestive of progress on several fronts. Although police corruption has remained generally stable at a high level, bribes paid to public servants in general have increased in recent years; *relative to bribes paid to all public servants*, police corruption appears to have fallen. We do not want to overstate this finding: We see no evidence that police corruption is actually falling. Numerous police reforms have been introduced at the federal, state, and municipal levels, and, although whether these reforms were implemented successfully is less clear and reforms can lack continuity, the types of reforms being introduced are ones consistent with the literature on incentive mechanisms for effective workforce management. Our empirical analysis of household data points to some positive indicators in terms of some of the key inputs that can affect police professionalization and performance. Education and pay levels of police have increased in recent years, though wage growth across age groups still remains relatively flat. Although these indicators of progress are encouraging, they must be assessed against a backdrop of continued drug violence in Mexico, kidnappings, and even wholesale firings of security personnel for corruption. Thus, it is clear that more progress is needed.

Recommendations

Recent police reforms are consistent with the types of reforms that the literatures on workforce management and corruption indicate are effective, and these policies should continue. Nonetheless, there is room for improvement. Of particular concern is the lack of continuity in reforms arising from the Mexican election system, in which politicians can serve only one term. Election turnover leads to new appointees and new reforms, and this cycle repeats. Previous research suggests that election continuity could reduce corruption and that Mexico should move toward seeking greater continuity in its reform efforts. This must be balanced, of course, with the need to remove corrupt employees from their positions; nevertheless, continuity of policies and incentives can coexist with changes in leadership or the workforce.

In addition, reforms lack coordination across municipalities and between municipalities, states, and the federal government. Greater coordination could improve the effectiveness of reforms. But coordination and centralization are not the same. In June 2010, Mexico's National Public Security Council agreed to unify the municipal police in Mexico under their respective states. Although such unification can improve coordination through better communication, care must be taken to ensure that concentrating police forces in the hands of a few institutions in this way does not lead to greater corruption.

Mexico's police reforms could also benefit from increased transparency and accountability stemming from better data collection and analysis by the government. Much of the data on crime, corruption, and law enforcement in Mexico are available, but only in an ad hoc form from private organizations. High quality publicly available data are needed to enable the public to audit and report on crime, corruption, and law enforcement on an ongoing basis. An independent commission should be appointed to identify the data that should be collected and maintained, who should maintain them, and what efforts would be required to ensure completeness, accuracy, and ease of availability. Furthermore, to eliminate the potential for corruption in the collection and reporting of data, an independent organization should be charged with auditing the data for accuracy.

Finally, more evidence is needed on the effectiveness of police reform efforts and on identifying ways to improve the reform process. We discuss a set of specific research initiatives that could be pursued to provide better data and to guide police reform. These studies include assessing recent municipal reform efforts, understanding the effects of political discontinuity on corruption, and surveying a nationally representative sample of Mexican police. Although the specific studies should be guided by the policy community, the key is that future efforts to combat police corruption in Mexico should include a plan to collect and analyze data on police activities and outcomes, which would increase transparency and improve policymaking.

Acknowledgments

The research in this report benefited from the help of several individuals and organizations. We would like to thank Emma Aguila, Timothy Bonds, Siddhartha Dalal, Debra Knopman, C. Richard Neu, Francisco Perez-Arce, Greg Ridgeway, K. Jack Riley, and James Thomson at RAND for their helpful comments. The report also benefited from the comments of our reviewers, Paul Heaton of RAND and Daniel Sabet of Georgetown University. We also are grateful to Emma Aguila for her help in accessing and interpreting Mexican household survey data. We benefited from useful discussions with Daniel Sabet about data and his ongoing research. We appreciate helpful responses from the Instituto Nacional de Estadística y Geografía (INEGI, or National Institute of Statistics and Geography) in Mexico regarding questions we had about its Encuesta Nacional de Ingresos y Gastos de los Hogares (National Survey of Income and Household Expenditure, or ENIGH) data sets. We thank Gabriela Martínez from the Banco de Información para la Investigación Aplicada en Ciencias Sociales (BIIACS, or Information Bank for Applied Research in Social Sciences) and Catalin Palmer from the Instituto Ciudadano de Estudios Sobre la Inseguridad (ICESI, or Citizens' Institute for Studies on Insecurity) for their feedback on obtaining and using data. Finally, we would like to thank RAND for supporting this research effort.

Abbreviations

AFI	Agencia Federal de Investigación, or Federal Investigation Agency
AVF	all-volunteer force
CALEA	Commission on Accreditation for Law Enforcement Agencies
CMO	la Clasificación Mexicana de Ocupaciones, or Mexican Classification of Occupations
CPI	Corruption Perceptions Index
ENCBG	Encuesta Nacional de Corrupción y Buen Gobierno, or National Survey on Corruption and Good Governance
ENIGH	Encuesta Nacional de Ingresos y Gastos de los Hogares, or National Survey of Income and Household Expenditure
ENSI	Encuesta Nacional Sobre Inseguridad, or National Survey on Insecurity
HSG	high school graduate
INEGI	Instituto Nacional de Estadística y Geografía, or National Institute of Statistics and Geography
LAPD	Los Angeles Police Department
PF	Policía Federal, or Federal Police
PFM	Policía Federal Ministerial, or Federal Ministerial Police
PFP	Policía Federal Preventiva, or Federal Preventive Police
PJF	Policía Judicial Federal, or Federal Judicial Police
PRI	Partido Revolucionario Institucional, or Institutional Revolutionary Party
SCIAN	el Sistema de Clasificación Industrial de América del Norte, or North American Industry Classification System
SSP	Secretaria de Seguridad Pública

SUBSEMUN   Subsidio de Seguridad Pública Municipal, or Subsidy for Municipal Public Security

TI   Transparency International

CHAPTER ONE

Introduction

It is widely acknowledged that corruption is rife within Mexico's security forces and judicial system (Reames, 2003; Morris, 1999). Corruption poses a threat to Mexico's national well-being by hampering economic growth and development and by compromising the security of its citizens. Although studies point to a long history of petty corruption in Mexico, the dramatic rise in recent years in the illicit drug trade and in weapon and human trafficking between Mexico and the United States have put a spotlight on how weak institutions hampered by corruption have exacerbated these problems (Meyer, 2007; Birns and Sánchez, 2007; Flakus, 2008). Consequently, many observers consider police corruption in Mexico a national security issue not only for Mexico but also for the United States (Schaefer, Bahney, and Riley, 2009; Chabat, 2006).

To strengthen institutions and root out corruption, the Mexican government has made reform of the security forces, particularly the police forces, a central component of its efforts. Police reform did not become a clear national priority until the 1990s, under the administration of Ernesto Zedillo (Sabet, 2010a), when a federal police force (known as the Federal Judicial Police [Policía Judicial Federal, or PJF] and later the Federal Preventive Police [Policía Federal Preventiva, or PFP]) was created to provide security in federal areas (such as highways) and coordinate with local authorities to prevent crimes and maintain order. Since then, numerous reforms have been proposed and implemented. These include restructuring and reorganizing the responsibilities of different police protection agencies at the federal, state, and municipal levels to enhance coordination and effectiveness, and strengthening municipal departments by setting new policies to improve funding, information technology, operations, and human resource management. Human resource management reforms have included policies to improve selection, screening, training, promotion, discipline, and compensation (Sabet, 2010b).

The police reforms are part of a larger, ongoing effort to the reform the law and justice system in Mexico. The aim of police reform efforts is to create a "new police model" that engenders professional police forces that are trustworthy and effective (Secretaría de Seguridad Pública, 2009; Ellingwood, 2009). In general, major reforms have been occurring at all levels (federal, state, and municipal) throughout the police forces and judicial system in Mexico for the past two decades (Sabet, 2010a, 2010b; E. Olson, 2009; Reames, 2003). And reforms are expected to continue.[1] Consequently, Mexico's policy environment is highly dynamic and continually changing when it comes to corruption and police reform.

In light of the national security implications of police corruption in Mexico and the central role of police reform in combating corruption, several key questions emerge:

- What types of reform does the available literature recommend? What is known about the roots of corruption, the factors affecting corruption, and the role of effective compensation and personnel management in mitigating corruption?
- What police reforms have been implemented in the past in Mexico?
- What is the available evidence on the impact of past reforms?

The purpose of this report is to provide information that helps address these policy questions. To answer the first question, we review past studies and analyses of corruption, focusing on the roles of economic and political institutions, incentives and compensation, and personnel management. We then draw insights on what the available literature considers effective corruption measures and human resource policies that lead to professional, trustworthy security forces.

We address the second question, on past reforms, by describing the historical context that led to calls for police reform and by briefly reviewing police reform efforts over the past 15 years at the federal, state, and municipal levels. We also identify how past and current reforms fit within the context of the literature on compensation and personnel management.

To address the third question, we combine results from recent studies on police reforms in Mexico with primary data analyses we conduct, drawing on numerous data sources on corruption and measures of inputs to police professionalism. Because the policy environment is dynamic, with multiple reforms occurring simultaneously, it is not possible to assess the effectiveness of individual reforms, at least not with existing, public data sources. Our approach is descriptive and uses several national data sets that include information on corruption perceptions, victimization, pay, education, and other demographic characteristics of the security forces in Mexico relative to other occupations to describe areas of improvement. Our analysis examines available information on trends in police corruption and provides some initial empirical evidence of increased professionalization of Mexico's police forces. Thus, the analysis is a first step.

We note three important potential limitations of our work. First, we approach the problem of corruption in the security forces from an explicitly economic perspective, something that we believe has not been emphasized in the existing literature. Our goal is to focus in particular on the incentives facing police that could tend to either promote or reduce corrupt activities. But our approach does not reflect the depth of institutional knowledge about Mexico, organized crime, and the police that exists in complementary studies by Mexican and non-Mexican scholars.

Second, to the extent possible, we incorporate quantitative data related to the concepts we discuss, especially corruption in Mexico and inputs to police and security force professionalism. The data we present are, to the best of our knowledge, the most comprehensive publicly

---

[1] For example, the National Public Security Council recently voted (in June 2010) to unify the 2,000 municipal police forces across Mexico into 32 new state police forces. Such a change, if it became law, would represent a dramatic change in how local-level protective services would be provided.

available data in Mexico. There are likely key administrative data that could be brought to bear on the topics and questions we discuss, but we do not have access to that information at present. In addition, much of the data should be interpreted cautiously—as we explain in more detail in Chapter Four—since we are considering difficult-to-measure concepts, such as corruption.

Finally, we want to be clear about the type of corruption on which we are focusing. Small-scale corruption, including petty bribery, low-level nepotism, and favoritism, is a serious issue in Mexico, and our analysis and recommendations are more relevant to this type of corruption than to any other. We do not focus on "grand corruption" perpetrated by high-level government officials, and we recognize that Mexico's severe and growing problem with drug-related crime has important implications for corruption as well. In giving only minor attention to these issues—especially narcotics-related crimes—we do not mean to imply that these issues are not as important as (or even more important than) low-level corruption, but they will likely require different solutions, which are beyond the scope of this report.

This report is organized as follows. Chapter Two provides information on the roots of corruption and the role of effective compensation and personnel management in stemming corruption. Chapter Three describes what police reforms have been implemented in the past and how they related to the literature summarized in Chapter Two. Chapter Four presents information related to what is known about the impact of police reforms. It reviews past studies and uses multiple household survey data sources to describe the current situation in Mexico with respect to corruption and the state of the security forces. We conclude in Chapter Five with an assessment of the kind of reforms that make sense in Mexico in light of the literature, past reforms, and available evidence on the current situation. The final chapter also recommends additional steps to improve data collection, which would enable better analysis of police reform in Mexico.

CHAPTER TWO

Insights from the Literature

Past studies provide insight into the factors that promote or facilitate corruption, the reforms that mitigate it, and the empirical evidence that supports these theories. Although relatively few studies provide direct evidence on the effectiveness of corruption-mitigating reforms, the larger literature points to key drivers and, therefore, the prime targets of reform. This chapter briefly reviews the literature on corruption—especially areas relevant to reducing corruption in the police—and the next chapter draws on this literature in our review of police reforms in Mexico.

Two related areas of study are relevant. The first concerns the macrolevel institutional context in which individual police officers make decisions about their involvement in corruption. If corruption is rampant among government leaders, and there is a culture of limited accountability, then—as described by Aidt (2003)—institutions are weak, and government officials who make and implement policy are not acting in the public interest. They cannot be counted on to create, implement, and enforce policies to induce police and other lower-level bureaucrats to avoid corruption. Within this institutional context, police department human resource policies that are intended to mitigate corrupt acts by individual officers are unlikely to be effective. Furthermore, the historical context of police reform, discussed in the next chapter, can be better understood by considering how institutional-level factors at the macro level can affect corruption at the micro level.

The second area concerns the microlevel decisionmaking of individual police officers. Even if corruption is relatively rare at the macro institutional level, at the micro level, individual police officers could have little incentive to avoid corruption. Aidt (2003) describes this situation as one in which a benevolent government official acts in the public interest but a nonbenevolent lower-level agent, such as a police officer, does not.

Our review of the literature addresses both the macro- and microlevel contexts. We first discuss the definition of the term *institution* and the literature on the broad factors leading to weak institutions, the context in which corruption is more likely to thrive. Weak institutions can limit the effectiveness of local policies intended to reduce corruption at the level of individual police officers, because government officials and policymakers cannot be trusted to implement and enforce those policies. We review the empirical evidence on the relationship between institutional strength and corruption. Because much of the literature on institutions does not focus specifically on corruption among police or other security forces, it provides only indirect information on the relationship between weak institutional factors and police corruption.

We next turn to the micro level and consider compensation and personnel management policies intended to professionalize the workforce. These policies are designed to influence the decision that individual police officers make to participate in corrupt activities, ignoring the institutional context. Many of the police reforms in Mexico, summarized in the next chapter, focus on improving compensation, selection, and other personnel management practices. The economics literature on human resource policy, known as *personnel economics*, considers the questions on the optimal human resource policies to attract and retain high caliber and qualified personnel, train them, motivate them to perform as required (and eschew corruption opportunities), assign and promote them to jobs for which they are best suited, and induce them to leave at the end of their career. Thus, this area of research is relevant to the reforms under way in Mexico. We consider this literature in the context of public sector organizations, focusing especially on compensation and personnel management policies to mitigate the incentives for malfeasance, though not necessarily corruption.[1] We supplement the discussion with empirical evidence on the effectiveness of such policies in one specific public security context—the U.S. military. We argue that this is a potentially useful example, though we acknowledge that the Mexican and U.S. contexts differ and that the military and police are different organizations.

We also discuss the economics literature pertaining to human resource policies and corruption, although not specifically police corruption. Much of this work concerns empirical evidence on the effect that higher pay can have on corruption. We also discuss the role of microlevel data in analyzing corruption. We conclude the chapter by summarizing the findings of the literature.

The Institutional Level

Institutions refers to the rules of society as they structure incentives in the political, social, or economic spheres (Acemoglu, Johnson, and Robinson, 2005). Ostrom (1986) defines institutions as rules or prescriptions that are commonly known and used by people to order repetitive and interdependent relationships, where *prescriptions* refers to the actions that are required, prohibited, or permitted. In game theory, *institutions* refers to the rules that define the structure of a game, affecting the actions that can be selected and the structure of incentives. In the context of a country's economy, *institutions* includes the structure and enforcement of property rights and the presence or absence of different market structures, thereby affecting economic incentives in society. For example, if people have exclusive property rights to the returns on their efforts, then they have a stronger incentive to invest, innovate, work hard, and generally engage in activities that increase those returns (Acemoglu, Johnson, and Robinson, 2005). Similarly, when markets exist and are perfectly competitive, resources are efficiently allocated to their highest use. Conversely, in the absence of property rights or markets, resources are misallocated, and people have little incentive to invest in physical or human capital or to take part in economic activities. In the context of a country's legal system, *institutions* includes the degree to which the rule of law matters and there is equality (or inequality) before the law. For example, equality before the law helps to ensure that there is an honest third party and permits enforcement of contracts and property rights.

---

[1] Although corruption and malfeasance are different phenomena, many of the insights from the personnel economics literature can be broadly applicable to the question of what policies might help combat corruption. Furthermore, we specifically consider the literature on incentives for corruption later in this chapter.

For the political arena, Acemoglu, Johnson, and Robinson (2005) differentiate between two types of political institutions. De jure institutions are the formal political institutions that influence the activities of politicians, including the form of government, such as democracy, dictatorship, autocracy, or constitutional monarchy. De facto institutions are groups that possess political power, even if not specified in a constitution. For example, these might be revolutionaries, peaceful protestors, lobbying groups, or others who use collective action to try to impose their wishes on society. The term *de facto institutions* also refers to what actually occurs versus what is supposed to occur. Rules and laws can be de jure and formally on the books, but, in reality, the de facto situation is that no one follows those rules and laws.

Widespread corruption at the macro level—for example, among policymakers, government officials, and even the general public—is the result, at least theoretically, of weak institutions. A question of particular interest, then, is what factors lead to weak institutions? Acemoglu, Johnson, and Robinson (2005) conclude that political institutions determine economic institutions because political institutions determine who holds power and those who hold power are the ones who define the economic rules of the game. Because those who hold power cannot credibly commit to how they will use (or abuse) their power once they have it, the tendency is for them to choose institutions that are most likely to benefit themselves, rather than the country as a whole. The result of monopoly political power is inefficient or corrupt institutions that do not provide broad, secure property rights to those without power. Consequently, institutions that lead to stagnated growth and more rampant corruption can benefit some groups. Similarly, institutions that promote growth might not necessarily benefit all groups in society. The key insight here is that the groups holding political power affect which institutions prevail.

Acemoglu, Johnson, and Robinson (2005) describe three necessary conditions for those who hold power to choose strong institutions. First, stronger economic institutions require constraints on the use of political power, such as a separation of powers between different power holders. Such an environment is more likely to produce secure property rights, instill equal justice before the law, and protect markets in which those who invest and contribute to economic activity earn the returns on those activities. Second, better institutions are likely to result when political power is in the hands of large and diverse groups in the population and includes those with access to the most important investment opportunities. If the political power base is very narrow, it is less likely to include those who need property right protection for major investments. Third, better economic institutions can arise only when there are limited opportunities to extract economic rents or to take advantage of corruption opportunities for those in a privileged position. For example, a country that has substantial natural wealth, such as petroleum or mineral reserves, is also a country with substantial economic rents. Having substantial national resources does not necessarily lead to weak institutions, but it does increase the incentives to those in power to engage in corrupt activities to extract those resources for their own benefit and reduces their incentives to relinquish or share power. We revisit these conditions in the next chapter in our discussion of the historical context of police reform and how broad political changes in Mexico also changed the institutional context in which corruption can occur.

Aidt (2003) also identifies discretionary power and economic rents among the necessary conditions for corruption to arise and persist. He argues that, when those in charge of implementing and designing institutions are not benevolent, corruption arises because power holders introduce inefficient policies that focus on extracting rents rather than on the public interest. From the standpoint of police corruption, this analysis implies that weak institutions prevent the human resource policies of the type discussed later in this chapter—those intended to induce officers and public employees in general to act in the public interest—from being implemented successfully.

Empirical Research on Institutions

Several studies have investigated empirically the relationship between institutions and corruption, often using cross-country macrolevel data. More recent studies use individual-level microdata. In both cases, the empirical literature provides only indirect evidence on how weak institutions affect police corruption, because most studies do not specifically focus on this form of corruption.

Woodruff (2006) provides an overview of empirical approaches to measuring institutions and their relationship with corruption. He finds that "formal institutions" have little effect on outcomes, while informal institutions matter. However, informal institutions—how laws are enforced in practice—are more difficult to measure, and measurements often rely on subjective assessments by experts or economic participants. Ades and Di Tella (1999) consider the effect that institutionally related variables, such as political rights or antitrust law, can have on corruption. They find that, although political freedoms are largely uncorrelated with corruption levels, countries with more effective antitrust laws tend to have less corruption. More recent work considers how the structure of government affects corruption. Gerring and Thacker (2004) estimate the relationship between territorial sovereignty and composition of the executive office on corruption and find that unitary and parliamentary political institutions are associated with lower levels of corruption.

A key institutional factor discussed above is political competition, which can serve as a check on political power. In early theoretical work, Shleifer and Vishny (1993) demonstrate that increased government competition can, under certain conditions, reduce corruption. However, when decentralization and competition lead to additional levels of government and increased regulation, corruption can increase, since there are more opportunities for government officials to extract bribes. In a review study on the relationship between government decentralization and corruption, Bardhan and Mookherjee (2006) find mixed results, with some studies suggesting that decentralization is associated with reduced corruption (Fisman and Gatti 2002), while other research finds little or no relationship—or, in some cases, a positive correlation—between decentralization, in the form of multiple levels of government, and corruption (Treisman, 2002). Recent microlevel work by Egel (2009) does little to clarify the relationship; he finds that tribal diversity has the opposite effect on corruption across regions as it does within regions and that recent decentralization reforms have no effect on patronage.

Another institutional feature that has received empirical attention is political oversight—mechanisms to reduce rent-seeking behavior. Olken (2007) uses microlevel data from a field experiment in Indonesia to assess the effect of government auditing systems on corruption in village road construction projects. He measures corruption by determining the discrepancy between reported and actual road construction expenditures; at the same time, he increases the audit likelihood for a randomly selected subset of construction projects. Government accountability, in the form of audits, reduced waste (interpreted in this context as corruption) by 4 percentage points. This compares favorably with having grassroots organizations participating in the oversight process, an alternative treatment that had little effect on corruption. Nevertheless, even when villages faced 100 percent audit likelihood (up from 4 percent pretreatment), 20 percent of expenditures were still unaccounted for. This suggests that even dramatic improvement in institutional quality and accountability is not sufficient to eliminate corruption.

A few empirical studies assess, largely through case studies, examples of effective institutional reform to reduce corruption. Drawing on the experiences of Hong Kong, India, and Indonesia, Palmier (1985) identifies three institutionally controlled factors that contribute to corruption: opportunities to act corruptly, public sector salaries, and the probability of detection and punishment. Quah (2001) applies this framework and chronicles the Singaporean government's success at moving from endemic corruption during the British colonial period to a country that is now consistently ranked among the least corrupt in the world.[2] He identifies key steps Singapore took to reduce corruption, including police corruption: adopting comprehensive, as opposed to incremental, anticorruption laws; implementing an autonomous anticorruption agency that is not housed within the police; and staffing anticorruption units with honest personnel who report to an "incorruptible" political leader.

Although amending laws and creating anticorruption commissions are some things most governments could do, ensuring political leaders' dedication to fighting corruption might not always be feasible. Indeed, in a comparative review of anticorruption policies in South Asia, Quah (1999) notes that both Singapore and Hong Kong were "blessed with political leaders who are determined to remove the problem of corruption" (p. 490). Focusing on another South Asian country, Malaysia, Siddiquee (2010) cites a lack of political commitment as the main cause of a lack of progress in fighting corruption, despite numerous institutional reforms and an "elaborate anti-corruption framework" (p. 168). The democratic process and political competition could help seat leaders who are dedicated to reform, although Singapore provides at least a partial counterexample.

Finally, the empirical literature also provides evidence on the role of nongovernmental institutions, especially the press, and the "checks" they provide on government behavior and corruption. Brunetti and Weder's (2003) analysis of cross-country data reveals a strong negative relationship between press freedom and corruption,[3] although press freedom is linked to other forms of institutional quality that can undermine its effectiveness (Djankov, Glaeser, et al., 2003). The limited microeconomic work on institutions and corruption supports the hypothesis that the press can serve to reduce corruption. In a series of papers on reducing corruption in the education sector in Uganda, Reinikka and Svensson (2004, 2005) show how a newspaper campaign to track public funds for schools reduced theft by local officials and politicians and improved education outcomes. They use proximity to a newspaper outlet as an instrument for exposure to the campaign and find that the campaign contributed to the 60 percentage point reduction in resource theft between 1995 and 2001. McMillan and Zoido (2004) examine bribe taking by the chief of Peru's secret police, Fladimiro Montesinos Torres, in the Fujimori administration. They find that the news media, particularly television, is the most forceful source of checks and balances underpinning democracy, measured in terms of the level of bribes required to gain cooperation. The highest bribes were paid to the television media, followed by bribes to politicians and judges.

---

[2] Singapore was ranked the third least-corrupt country in the world in 2009, according to Transparency International (2009).

[3] Using similar data, Lederman, Loayza, and Soares (2005) find similarly beneficial effects of press freedoms.

Policies at the Level of the Individual Decisionmaker

At the level of the individual police officer, human resource policies can influence the incentives that lead qualified people to join an organization, to stay, to be productive and direct effort toward the organization's goals, to seek out leadership positions, and to eventually leave. The personnel economics literature is concerned with the optimal human resource policies of organizations, especially those designed to mitigate the incentive for malfeasance and "slacking off" and for inducing the best-qualified people to self-select into the organization and into leadership positions (Lazear, 1995; Lazear and Gibbs, 2009).

We review recent studies that examine these policies in the public sector context, and we begin by focusing on performance-incentive mechanisms or, more broadly, the policies that induce employees to take actions consistent with their organization's goals.[4] Studies typically find that pay-for-performance mechanisms that work in the private sector are not feasible in the public sector (Dixit, 2002). Our review considers the reasons for the disconnect between private and public sector solutions and discusses the literature on alternative mechanisms or policies. In the process, it reviews key insights from the personnel economics literature on promotion, compensation policy, accountability mechanisms, and other policies intended to attract, retain, motivate, and select personnel. Because personnel economics considers broader issues than corruption, we also review the literature on incentives for corruption. In the remainder of this chapter, we ignore the institutional context by assuming that institutions are relatively strong to the extent that property rights are secure and a third party (e.g., the courts) can and does reasonably enforce human resource policies.

Personnel Economics Literature

Much of the research on personnel economics is concerned with incentive mechanisms, a topic also known as the *principal–agent* problem. In the context of the employment relationship—such as an individual police officer employed by a municipal, state, or federal police force—the principal is the employer and the agent is the employee. The basic principal–agent problem is that each side has distinct objectives or misaligned incentives, and the question is what incentive mechanism(s) the principal can efficiently design to induce the agent to have the same objectives as the principal. In the public sector context, the basic principal–agent incentive problem is that the objective of the principal is to support the public interest—in the case of the police chief, fighting crime—while the agent (for example, a street-level cop) wants to pursue private interests, such as maximizing compensation from all sources, including bribes.

The usual solution to the basic principal–agent problem is a pay-for-performance compensation scheme that sets pay at a level proportional to the agent's output, where *output* is easily defined.[5] However, pay-for-performance schemes are not commonly used in the government sector, and, even in cases where they are used, relatively little compensation is at risk of being lost for poor performance. First, public interest objectives are usually complex and multi-dimensional (Tirole, 1994; Dixit, 2002). For example, the objectives of a police department are numerous and include law enforcement, protecting the public, successful investigation of crimes, and prosecution of criminals. Second, the objectives can be difficult to define in a way

---

[4]   Reviews of this literature can also be found in Prendergast (1999), Dixit (2002), and Burgess and Ratto (2003).

[5]   In the basic principal–agent model, the agent's output is either perfectly measurable (but only if the principal incurs a monitoring cost) or the principal can measure only average or expected output, not actual output.

that makes it easy to determine whether they have been met (Wilson, 1989; Dewatripont, Jewitt, and Tirole, 1999). Sometimes, the principal is difficult to identify, or there might be more than one principal (Dixit, 2002). For example, in a government bureaucracy, the principal could be the President, Congress, the head of the specific bureaucracy, or, more narrowly, multiple middle-level managers within the bureaucracy. Third, in the public sector, whether an agent is performing consistently with the principal's objectives might be difficult to measure (Holmstrom and Milgrom, 1991). For example, the objective of a police officer might be crime prevention, a concept that is difficult to define in a way that can be easily and completely measured.

Another reason for the absence of pay-for-performance schemes in the public sector is that public sector output is often the result of team effort, making it difficult to measure an agent's individual contribution to overall output. Holmstrom (1982) shows that, when individual effort is difficult to detect, team effort can lead to free-riding problems, in which each member of the team "free-rides" on the efforts of his or her teammates.

When agent performance is difficult to measure, it is often assessed in the form of subjective performance evaluations, though quantitative metrics can also be used, if available. The advantage of subjective evaluation is that evaluators can account for ill-defined dimensions of performance. However, subjective evaluations can also have unintended consequences: The accuracy of the assessment can be subject to error; the accuracy cannot be fully verified by outsiders; and the subjectivity of these evaluations can lead to evaluator favoritism or to employee lobbying. Furthermore, the evaluator might have an incentive to be lenient or to give overly positive assessments if doing so minimizes employee complaints about the evaluation process, and the evaluator faces no penalties in the form of lower pay for inaccurate assessments. The problem of lenient ratings is evident in the civil service by the common problem of "grade inflation," in which nearly all employees get top ratings. For example, Asch (2005) shows that more than 85 percent of General Schedule federal employees in the U.S. Department of Defense in 1996 received either a 1 or 2 (the top ratings) on a rating scale of 1 to 5. Prendergast (1999) shows that subjective performance ratings tend to be compressed in the private sector as well and that the compression becomes more severe as ratings become more important for setting pay.

Because of unintended consequences, explicit pay-for-performance incentive schemes are rarely used in the public sector. Instead, it is more common to find promotion systems, systems based on seniority (such as pay bands), accountability systems, and mechanisms to attract and retain high caliber people in public sector organizations. These policies can address not only the principal–agent problem of motivating employees but also questions of how to set pay and personnel policies to attract, retain, train, promote, and eventually separate personnel. In the rest of this section, we focus on the questions of motivation, recruitment, and retention.

Promotion Systems. Promotion systems are personnel policies in which pay levels associated with different grades or ranks are specified in advance, such as in a published pay table, and an employee moves up the ranks or grades if his or her performance is better than that of his or her peers in the same rank or grade. Promotion usually means a job change as well as a change in pay and occurs only if a job opening is available in the higher grade. Theoretically, promotion-based personnel systems, together with meaningful pay changes, align incentives and induce the same effort levels as explicit pay-for-performance schemes (Lazear and Rosen, 1981). Obviously, if promotions are not based on performance but on favoritism, then the incentive effect of the promotion system is diluted.

Promotion systems are quite common in the public sector in the United States, in part because they address some of the unintended consequences associated with pay-for-performance systems. First, measuring output for promotion determination is easier than for a pay-for-performance scheme because the evaluator only has to compare output among employees (whose output is higher?) and does not have to measure the absolute level of output. Second, promotion systems can reduce unexpected variability in employee earnings caused by random external factors, such as the state of the general economy, if those factors are common to all workers competing for promotion. For example, if a weak economy affects all employees' performance in the same way and is the major component of random variations in performance, a ranking of employees' performance for promotion purposes nets out the adverse effects of the economy on performance because all employees faced the same weak economy. Third, the common pay table used as part of the promotion system helps ensure the transparency and credibility of the compensation system to the extent that it is common knowledge among employees. If pay levels at different grades are common knowledge, the employer cannot secretly renege and withhold pay raises when the employee is promoted. Reneging is a drawback of explicit pay-for-performance systems when performance is difficult to verify by a third party. In this case, the employer can always claim in a court of law that the employee failed to perform (Prendergast, 1999).

Promotion systems also have drawbacks. First, employees have an incentive to engage in "influence activities," in which they attempt to influence the promotion outcomes either by lobbying the supervisor who makes the promotion decision or by sabotaging (or spreading incorrect rumors about the performance of) "competitors" who are also vying for promotion. These activities divert employees' attention and time from productive work. The U.S. military solves the problem of influence activities by relying on anonymous national selection boards for some groups of officers. The problem of sabotage is ameliorated because service members compete against "the national field," which is made up of all eligible members, who remain anonymous for the most part and are scattered throughout the world. But in situations in which promotions draw from a local pool of employees, each employee eligible for promotion is acquainted with both the supervisor making the promotion system and his or her competitors, thereby making influence activities more likely. Another potential drawback of promotions is that supervisors might use promotion to solve personnel problems. For example, supervisors might promote individuals who are difficult to work with as a way of removing them from the workgroup and sending them elsewhere without having to fire them.

Promotion schemes are often found in hierarchical organizations. Research finds that, in the optimal pay structure, pay levels should be "skewed," with the differences in pay across hierarchical levels rising with level (Rosen, 1982). That is, the difference in pay between the top two levels should be larger than the difference in pay between the two levels just below them. The pay gain associated with each successive promotion must rise to maintain the same expected financial incentive in order to discourage malfeasance. Given that individuals have fewer remaining promotions left in their career as they climb the promotion ladder and that the probability of promotion also usually declines as one moves up the ranks, the expected financial incentive to supply effort falls as each person's career progresses. The gain in pay associated with promotion must therefore rise at higher ranks to offset the negative effect on effort as people move up the ranks. Higher-ranked jobs also usually involve greater responsibility, so poorer performance, corruption, or malfeasance in these jobs can have wider-ranging negative effects on the organization. The pay gain associated with each promotion must increase to induce the most-talented workers to stay in the organization and to seek advancement to the senior ranks, at which their ability is the most valuable.

Promotions are the main tool used to reward performance in the U.S. military. Asch and Warner (1994, 2001) use a simulation model of the Army's personnel to estimate the effects that changing pay and promotion can have on the performance and retention of high caliber soldiers and find that larger pay spreads across ranks motivate better performance and retain higher-quality people. The study finds that a skewed pay raise for military members in which those in higher ranks get higher pay raises results in substantially greater performance, and at less cost.

As discussed in the next chapter, one of the aims of Mexican police reforms is to implement a successful merit-based promotion system. The incentive literature implies that, for a promotion system to be successful in motivating performance and developing future leaders, promotions should be based on merit relative to others also under consideration for promotion. Pay raises associated with promotion should be skewed (rising with rank), the pay table should be widely disseminated so that everyone knows what raises they can expect in the future, and the police chief should not be able to renege and fail to give a pay raise once an officer has been promoted. Finally, promotions and the pay raises associated with promotion should not be subject to favoritism or the lobbying efforts of those vying for promotion. This means that the promotion process must be transparent and the results subject to audit. One step toward transparency is to publish the pay table and promotion results.

Seniority-Based Systems. In seniority-based pay systems, pay is set to increase with additional seniority or years of service within the organization. The literature offers two approaches to structure pay to ensure aligned incentives. Lazear (1979) argues that pay over a career should be structured so that employees are underpaid relative to their productive worth during the initial phase of their career, but later, when they are more senior, they are overpaid relative to their worth (and external pay opportunities)—but only if they demonstrate high performance in the initial phase of their career. If they do not demonstrate adequate performance (for example, by engaging in corruption), they should be fired, thereby forfeiting the promised higher future overpayment later in their career. Thus, there is a "speed bump," or control point, during the career, beyond which an employee is not allowed to continue to work for the organization without having demonstrated adequate performance. In this scheme, pay over the employee's career grows faster than productivity, but only high-performing junior employees are permitted to stay.[6]

The second approach recognizes that employees have postservice career concerns and care how performance in their current job affects their future job opportunities outside the organization. If good performance in the current job leads to better future external job offers, employees have an incentive to work in a manner consistent with the principal's objectives, even in the absence of explicit pay-for-performance contracts and even if they do not end up eventually changing jobs (Fama, 1980).[7] For career concerns to motivate people to refrain from

---

[6]   One problem with this incentive scheme is that employees have no incentive to separate or retire when they are senior employees, because they are being paid more than their productive worth. Lazear (1979, 1983) discusses how mandatory retirement and non–actuarially fair pensions are important mechanisms to induce employees to retire involuntarily (as in the case of mandatory retirement) or voluntarily (as in the case of non–actuarially fair pensions).

[7]   As discussed in Holmstrom (1982), a problem with using career concerns as part of an incentive mechanism is that junior employees will work too hard (when the external market is still making judgments about their performance and their entire

corruption or to perform well, external job opportunities must recognize and reward honesty and good performance in the current job. Put another way, employees must be able to develop reputations (positive or negative) that follow them across employers.

Tirole (1994) discusses the importance of career concerns as a method of providing incentives in the public sector and notes that civil service personnel, especially political appointees, are often more concerned about the effect of their current performance on future job prospects in both the government and the private sector than they are about job projects in their current job. Drawing from earlier work by Holmstrom (1982), Tirole lists the four conditions necessary for career concerns in government to be an effective method of motivating high performance: (1) Performance on any given task must be visible; (2) current performance must provide information about productivity in future tasks; (3) individuals must care about future outcomes (i.e., they must not discount future outcomes too much); and (4) both the external and internal markets must be able to learn about individual performance at a fairly low cost. These conditions make clear that the employee's reputation plays an important role. Employees who gain a reputation for poor performance or for corruption reduce their chances of getting a good future job in honest organizations. For example, the U.S. military gives poor performers a "dishonorable discharge." Having such a discharge on one's employment record conveys information to future prospective employers that the person's performance while in service was substandard. Consequently, military members know that, if they care about their postservice employment opportunities, they must perform at a level that ensures an honorable discharge. By the same token, organizations can earn a bad reputation for reneging on pay or treating employees poorly, thereby hurting their ability to hire high-performing workers in the future. If hiring high quality employees is important, the organization has an incentive to refrain from such behavior.

More broadly, the literature points to the importance of a well-considered career–pay profile in which pay grows with job and labor force experience as an employee becomes more productive. The pay profile can increase work incentives and incentives to be honest and avoid corruption, as long as employees who fail to be productive are terminated, thereby forgoing the opportunity to earn higher pay in the future. As is discussed in the next chapter, recent police reforms in Mexico focus on raising pay. The literature points to the importance of not only the level of pay but also the structure of pay over the course of a career and the importance of personnel policies, such as termination for unproductive employees.

Although the discussion here has focused on pay profiles as a work incentive, the literature also points to rising pay over the career to motivate employees to invest in both general and job-specific skills, with the anticipation of receiving higher pay in the future, reflecting their higher productivity.

Accountability Mechanisms. Prendergast (2001) considers the role of oversight, a type of auditing mechanism commonly used in the public sector. He shows that police departments and other public agencies that confer benefits, or dole out penalties (such as arrests), must choose between relying on internal oversight mechanisms versus external ones. Internal

---

career spans before them) and senior employees will work too little (because the market has already made its judgment and these workers have little of their career left before retirement). Gibbons and Murphy (1992) show that the optimal incentive scheme over workers' careers will involve a heavier reliance on career concerns and nonexplicit pay-for-performance schemes for junior and midcareer workers but a weaker reliance on career concerns for senior workers. In fact, the optimal scheme for senior workers will rely more heavily on explicit pay-for-performance incentive schemes because career concerns are less relevant when there is little concern about external job opportunities.

oversight methods are subject to bias because government officials are relatively unwilling to investigate and discipline wrongdoing among government employees. On the other hand, an internal auditor is more likely than an external auditor is to have more inside knowledge of how things work. Audits by less informed external third parties, such as the media and the public, are more likely to be unbiased, but government employers can change their actions to "stay out of the limelight" and underperform.

Prendergast provides evidence of the effect of external oversight using data from the Los Angeles Police Department (LAPD). Following a major LAPD scandal in the mid-1990s, the LAPD responded by improving the public's ability to make complaints against police officers and by investigating all complaints. Prendergast finds that officers responded to increased public oversight by cutting down on actions that could lead to an investigation, such as reducing the number of arrests, use of force per arrest, and the general "level of aggressiveness" in pursuing possible criminals. Shi (2009) finds similar evidence from the Cincinnati, Ohio, police department. Following a 2001 race riot following the shooting of an unarmed African American teen by a white police officer, media attention for the Cincinnati Police Department increased sharply. Shi shows that officers responded to the increased public attention by cutting down on arrests, especially the types of arrests that are most likely to be error-prone, such as drug-law violations.

Incentives to Attract and Retain Talent. Another goal of human resource policies is to attract and retain high caliber personnel with high aptitudes and better education. As we discuss in the next chapter, one of the aims of Mexican police reforms is to raise pay to attract better-qualified applicants.

Pay for performance is one approach to attracting talented workers, who are attracted to such systems because they can expect higher-than-average earnings. Another approach is to use apprenticeship or internship programs (Guasch and Weiss, 1981; Lazear, 1986), in which pay is set far below the apprentice's productive worth in order to discourage poorly qualified applicants. In the postapprenticeship career, pay for highly qualified applicants is set high enough to offset the low pay earned in the apprenticeship period.

Another approach is for the organization to set pay higher than what employees can expect to earn in other jobs, using "efficiency wages" to increase the size and average quality of the applicant pool from which it can draw (Weiss, 1980). This can also boost the average quality of the personnel organizations retain. The U.S. federal government has used this approach since the mid-1970s. Borjas (2002) finds that the real earnings of male full-time, full-year workers in the federal government exceeded those of private sector male workers with similar human-capital characteristics, such as education, although the earning gap has declined. Various studies have also examined the distribution of earnings in the federal and private sectors. Borjas (2002), Gibbs (2001), and Katz and Krueger (1991) all argue that the compressed structure of earnings among those in the federal civil service relative to those in the private sector will likely hurt the federal sector's ability to recruit and retain highly talented personnel in the future. Thus, U.S. public sector workers at the federal level tend to be paid more than their private sector counterparts with similar background characteristics, although the pay variance across workers is less than in the private sector.

For police agencies to attract and retain qualified, high caliber personnel, compensation must be competitive, though not necessarily the same as nonpolice compensation. To assess pay competitiveness, it is important to consider metrics related to the quality and qualifications of those who apply, are hired, and stay in service—not necessarily to compare pay levels. These findings suggest that recent police reforms in Mexico that raise pay for high quality hires are likely to help improve the quality of those who enter and stay in the police forces. Although the empirical evidence on whether paying efficiency wages reduces corruption is not conclusive, recent efforts to raise police pay in Mexico are consistent with providing an incentive to avoid corruption.[8]

An Example of Compensation Policies: The U.S. Military

The U.S. military is a substantially different organization from a local-, state-, or even federal-level police force in Mexico. It has a different institutional context, set of missions, organizational structure, and constraints. Nonetheless, the U.S. military's approach to compensation and personnel management provides a useful example of effective human resource policies for a public sector security-oriented workforce that could inform the development of similar policies in other security-oriented organizations, such as the police. Furthermore, substantial research is available on the military's policies and their effectiveness, research that is generally unavailable for police and could provide insights for police forces, including Mexico's, about lessons learned, albeit in a different organizational context.[9]

In 1973, the United States eliminated military conscription, and, since then, it has had to develop policies to support an all-volunteer force (AVF), including attracting and retaining high quality military personnel, training them, motivating strong performance, promoting and assigning them to positions for which they are best suited, and eventually separating them at the end of a successful career. The AVF in the United States is widely viewed by policymakers, the public, and the media as a resounding success.

Like other public sector organizations, the military does not use pay-for-performance schemes to motivate performance and induce higher-quality personnel to enter and stay in service. Rather, it relies on a compensation system with several key components. The foundation of the system is monthly basic pay, given in a published pay table in which pay for a member depends on his or her current rank (or grade) and years of service in the military. Congress increases basic pay annually, usually as an across-the-board increase for all members, to reflect overall changes in average wages in the U.S. economy. Military members receive individual basic pay raises as they gain additional years of service or are promoted to a higher rank.

Numerous studies of the U.S. military find that raising pay is highly effective in increasing the supply of high caliber recruits to the military (Hosek, Warner, and Asch, 2007; Asch, Heaton, et al., 2010). The effect of pay (and other factors that affect recruiting) are measured as an *elasticity*, a term taken from the economics literature. The pay elasticity is defined as the percentage increase in high caliber recruits associated with a 1 percent increase in military pay. Asch, Heaton, et al. (2010) use data covering the period 2000 to 2008 and estimate a pay elasticity of 1.2 for the Army and 0.7 for the Navy, meaning that a 1 percent increase in military pay relative to civilian pay is estimated to increase high caliber recruits in the Army by 1.2 percent and in the Navy by 0.7 percent.

---

[8]   As noted previously and discussed in the section on institutions and in Chapter Four, however, the benefits of higher pay strongly depend on credible enforcement of anticorruption laws and policies; higher pay without the threat of punishment will likely have a limited effect on bribery and corruption.

[9]   To gain insight about policy effects, studies of U.S. military personnel policy sometimes draw from police departments' experiences. (See, most recently, National Defense Research Institute, 2010.)

Research also shows that higher military pay also is effective in retaining military personnel (Warner and Asch, 1995; Goldberg, 2001; Hansen and Wenger, 2002). These studies focus on the retention decisions of those who have completed their service obligation and so are free to leave the military.[10] For example, Hansen and Wenger (2002) use Navy data from the 1990s and estimate a pay elasticity of 1.6, meaning that a 1 percent increase in military pay, relative to civilian pay, increases the probability that those who have completed their service obligation will stay in the military by 1.6 percent.

Although military pay is the main policy used to attract and retain high caliber people, promotions are the main tool used to reward performance over the course of a career with promotion timing and the structure of pay across ranks in the pay table determining the reward level. As discussed earlier, Asch and Warner (1994, 2001) estimate the effects that changing pay and promotion can have on the performance and retention of high caliber soldiers and find that a skewed pay raise results in substantially greater performance and is more efficient, raising performance for the same cost and retention outcomes.

The U.S. military also relies on "special and incentive pays." The purpose of these pays is to provide military managers flexibility to target pay toward members with critical skills that are difficult to recruit or retain (such as combat arms), who have skills or are in locations that involve unusual or hazardous duty (such as demolition specialists), or who require substantial training (such as pilots). Among the most important special and incentive pays are deployment-related pays, particularly those related to duty in hazardous locations (such as Iraq and Afghanistan) and recruitment- and retention-related bonuses. These pays are targeted to specific personnel and are turned on and off as conditions change. For example, when recruiting and retention improve, the military slashes its recruiting and retention bonuses.

Numerous studies have found that bonuses help recruiting and retention, especially in hard-to-fill critical skills. Asch, Heaton, et al. (2010) estimate a bonus enlistment elasticity of 0.2 for the Army and 0.1 for the Navy. Thus, bonuses have a modest effect on enlistments. The effect is smaller than the effect of a pay increase because pay increases are across the board and increase pay over the entire career while bonuses are a one-time cash benefit. On the other hand, studies find that bonuses have a much larger effect on channeling recruits into hard-to-fill occupations. Polich, Dertouzos, and Press (1986) find that offering a bonus increases the number of recruits in critical occupations by 30 to 40 percent, holding constant the total number of recruits. Similarly, studies find that expanding reenlistment bonuses is also effective (Asch, Heaton, et al., 2010; Hosek and Martorell, 2009; Hogan et al., 2005; Moore et al., 2007); they increase both the number of people who choose to stay in the military and the length of time each one stays.

Though widely viewed as successful, the human resource policies of the U.S. military are not without criticism. However, much of the criticism is focused on how to improve the effectiveness, efficiency, flexibility, or equity of a system that is already viewed as generally working well. The policies are generally not focused on whether the current system embeds incentives for corruption or other wrongdoing, though some recent research does address this issue among general flag officers (Harrell and Hix, forthcoming) and among military recruiters (Asch and Heaton, 2010). Although not a perfect analogy, the experience of the U.S. military

---

[10] People who enlist in the U.S. military sign an enlistment contract that stipulates that they must serve for a specific number of years, usually between three and six years, depending on the occupation and service. Once the contract is fulfilled, enlisted personnel can reenlist by signing a new contract.

suggests that public sector compensation and personnel policies can be effective in professionalizing a security force.

Incentives for Corruption

Becker and Stigler's (1974) early theoretical work on corruption established the link between worker compensation and bribe taking. Under certain assumptions, such as third-party enforcement or credible threat of punishment, paying employees higher "efficiency" wages above what they could earn in alternative employment outside the police force can reduce bribes by increasing the potential cost, in the form of lost wages, of taking a bribe. That is, if a corrupt law enforcer is fired, he or she experiences a cost in the form of lower wages or, possibly, unemployment. In practice, however, this relationship is difficult to establish empirically. Using cross-country analysis, Treisman (2000) finds little to no evidence that higher wages reduce corruption, and, although Van Rijckeghem and Weder (2001) find that wages are correlated with lower corruption, the magnitude of their results is discouraging from a policy perspective.[11]

More recent work by Di Tella and Schargrodsky (2003) uses administrative data on hospital purchases, wages, and auditing in Argentina and finds more compelling evidence of a negative relationship between wages and corruption. Their result holds, however, only under intermediate—not the highest—levels of auditing. Although they do not establish the effect of wages on bribe taking, Gorodnichenko and Peter (2007) use microdata from Ukraine to provide strong suggestive evidence that public sector employees who are paid less than their private sector counterparts supplement their income through bribery.

Case studies have also made the link between salaries and corruption, suggesting that higher wages have been an important part of anticorruption efforts (Palmier, 1985). Quah (1999) notes that many countries with significant corruption problems, including Indonesia, Thailand, the Philippines, and Singapore, had or have public sector salaries that are quite low. In the case of Singapore, government officials raised salaries, but, due to budget constraints, the major wage increases occurred two decades after the government implemented other reforms. Thus, it is difficult to draw strong conclusions about the role of salaries from the limited number of attempts at salary reform.

A different strand of the literature considers the relationship between wages and corruption using data from laboratory experiments to better control for confounding factors that make observational research difficult. Jacquemet (2005) looks at wage effects on corruption in a laboratory experiment and finds that higher wages are associated with lower bribery rates; however, the experiment also addresses reciprocity and fairness issues, which could drive the result and are difficult to assess in real-life settings. Azfar and Nelson (2007) find similar results in a laboratory experiment that looks at embezzlement by executives in a firm setting. Despite the benefits of a controlled "experimental" environment, however, it is difficult to assess the external validity of these results. Another study, by Barr, Lindelow, and Serneels (2004), uses Ethiopian health workers to attempt to improve the external validity of their experiments; they find that higher wages have a small but positive effect on reducing corruption.

Government policies can also discourage corruption through nonmonetary incentives. An example is the prevalence of freedom of information laws and asset disclosure provisions

---

[11] Specifically, Van Rijckeghem and Weder find that even an increase in wages of 100–200 percent would have a relatively modest impact on reducing corruption (as measured by a well-known corruption index).

for public officials. Djankov, La Porta, et al. (2010) review the asset disclosure laws for 175 countries and find evidence that such rules can put downward pressure on corruption, as captured by standard subjective measures. However, it is difficult to assess the causal relationship between government policies and corruption, since less corrupt countries might be more likely to implement or enforce existing laws than are more corrupt countries.

The Role of Data and the Analytical Approach to Studying Incentives

We conclude our literature review by noting that the recent empirical analyses of corruption and studies of incentives rely on high quality microlevel data and use analytical methods that focus on individual decisionmakers rather than aggregate cross-country comparisons. Such data and methods are preferred because they permit better or even causal estimates of policy effects, thereby informing policymakers about effective reforms. In contrast, research that relies on case studies or aggregate-level data provide, at best, information on correlations between outcomes and policies and are subject to aggregation biases, in which estimates of policy effects on outcomes reflect changes in the composition of the aggregate group rather than changes in outcomes resulting from policy.

Higher-quality studies of incentives in organizations generally use administrative data on each employee in the organization over some segment of his or her career; in some cases, they use survey data that are representative of the organization's employees. Analysis methods vary across studies but usually involve estimating statistical models of individual decisionmaking by employees. For instance, studies of the effects that pay has on retention use data on the individual retention decisions of each employee and estimate the effects of pay, controlling for other factors affecting the retention decision, such as the state of the economy.

Similarly, recent studies of corruption rely on similar modeling approaches. For example, the Di Tella and Schargrodsky (2003) study mentioned earlier uses administrative data on individual hospital purchases, audit results, and wages. Benjamin Olken's work in Indonesia relies on both microeconomic data (2006) and experimental methods (2007) to estimate the effects of corruption and assess programs designed to reduce it.

To date, much of the research on Mexico's police and security forces relies on aggregate data analysis or case study. In Chapter Five, we discuss areas for future research on corruption among Mexico's security forces. Much of this research would be best conducted using microlevel data.

Summary

Institutions refer to the "rules" that govern political, administrative, legal, and economic activity. Three conditions are necessary for strong institutions to be chosen by those in power. These include a broad base of political power, relatively few opportunities to extract rents from society's resources, and constraints on the use (and abuse) of power. Theoretically, the prevalence of weak institutions not only lead to greater macrolevel corruption but hamper the implementation of effective human resource policies targeted to police officers. Empirical analysis, mostly relying aggregate cross-country data, shows some evidence that factors related to weak institutions are associated with more corruption. For example, studies find evidence to support the notion that freedom of the press is associated with less corruption, as is auditing. Case studies from several countries indicate the importance of comprehensive reform efforts, rather than an incremental approach, and the necessity of strong political leadership supporting reform. These studies provide some evidence that the macrolevel institutional context matters for mitigating corruption, though not specifically police corruption.

At the micro level, the literature provides insights on the benefits of aligning public employee incentives with the public interest and on effective compensation and personnel management policies. Implementing pay-for-performance mechanisms is challenging in the public sector because of issues related to multiple objectives, multiple principals, performance measurement, and the teamwork setting, among others. For example, pay for performance for police officers would be problematic because pay based on any easily measured metric of performance, such as numbers of arrests, could easily lead to abuse as officers increase arrests to increase their pay.

The literature points to other mechanisms to embed incentives for performance and to hold employees accountable, including pay levels, promotion systems, career concerns, other methods of varying pay with seniority, and auditing mechanisms. The research shows the importance of setting compensation at a competitive level to attract and retain high quality personnel, of designing a merit-based promotion system that appropriately structures promotion-inducing pay raises to maintain effort incentives over the career, of setting pay to vary with seniority in a way that recognizes increasing skill and incentives over the career, and finally of the role of auditing mechanisms, such as internal and external oversight. However, each approach has advantages and potential drawbacks. For example, available evidence shows that external oversight can lead officers to cut back on arrests and other actions that put them "in the limelight."

Setting up proper incentives for police might require multiple policies working in concert, rather than a single policy, such as pure auditing, that might produce perverse results. Ichniowski, Shaw, and Prennushi (1997) find that multiple incentive schemes had a larger effect on worker productivity than single schemes used alone. The implication is that a comprehensive set of multiple policies, rather than a single policy, is more likely to be effective.

The next chapter reviews police reforms in Mexico and draws from the literature to assess whether reforms are consistent with the insights from the literature.

CHAPTER THREE

Mexico's Police Reforms

This chapter reviews past police reforms in Mexico, drawing from the literature review in the previous chapter to understand whether these reforms seem sensible. We begin by summarizing briefly Mexico's political history and past police reforms—in particular, some of the events that led to a push for police reform. The chapter then describes the structure of police forces in Mexico and describes police reform efforts targeted to the federal, municipal, and state levels. It also describes reforms specifically related to police compensation and personnel policies, including pay, selection, and training aimed at professionalizing the Mexican police.

Historical Context

In the aftermath of the Mexican Revolution between 1910 and 1917, the Institutional Revolutionary Party (Partido Revolucionario Institucional, or PRI) emerged as the dominating political force in Mexico in the 20th century. The PRI regime was characterized by a strong presidency and an authoritarian one-party system with high levels of corruption and a deficient judicial system (Chabat, 2006). Political competition was limited, with election results predetermined. PRI exerted control not just on political institutions but also on economic institutions and society. Bureaucrats had wide discretion and ability to abuse their authority. On the other hand, as described by Morris (2007), corruption aided PRI's political stability and continuity over this period by ensuring loyalty to the president and enforcing adherence to the existing system. In the context of the literature review in the previous chapter, the political dominance of PRI for much of the 20th century and the widespread corruption led to weak economic and judicial institutions in Mexico.

The political context began to shift in the 1980s, leading to a crisis of legitimacy for PRI and a deteriorating political system. The 1982 debt crisis precipitated an economic decline in Mexico that included lower wages, higher unemployment, and a lower standard of living for Mexico's citizens. The security environment also changed, with a growing refugee population from Guatemala, El Salvador, and elsewhere, as people fled unstable countries affected by revolutionary movements in Central America. These changes set the stage for growing protests and social movements that eroded the PRI political base, led to policies that opened the previously closed Mexican economy to freer trade, and helped liberate controls over business, the press, and civil society. The deterioration of the political system also led to a dramatic rise in drug trafficking and drug-related corruption that began in the mid- to late 1980s (Morris, 1999). The literature on institutions reviewed in the previous chapter suggests that the debt crisis of the 1980s and the weakened economy led to the growth of opposition parties, what Acemoglu,

Johnson, and Robinson (2005) call de facto political institutions because, although they did not hold formal power, working together, they were able to influence change and broaden their political power base.

The 1990s were marked by both a rise in corruption and new efforts to curb corruption. The Zedillo administration (1994–2000) introduced numerous reforms. These reforms accelerated with the watershed end of the PRI monopoly on the presidency in 2000. In that year, Vicente Fox, of the opposition National Action Party (Partido Acción Nacional, or PAN), was elected. The new administration made public security a priority, with reforming the public security system and fighting corruption as key steps in the strategy to improve security. The presidential election of the opposition party culminated the exertion of the power of the de facto political groups, as described in the previous chapter, a shift that helped create a broader power base in Mexico. This is one of the conditions that are likely to lead to stronger institutions.

Since the 1990s, many reforms to the judicial, public security, and police systems have occurred, representing the growth of stronger institutions. For example, efforts to modernize and professionalize the police forces, described next in this chapter, can be seen as efforts to help secure property rights for Mexican citizens. Reforms that seek to standardize and modernize police operations, professionalize the police force through clearly articulated civil service systems, and impart better oversight through data collection can be considered efforts to limit the use of power by those with power.

On the other hand, numerous police reforms have sought to consolidate power. For example, in 2009, the PFP, with the new name Policía Federal, or Federal Police (PF), became part of the Secretaria de Seguridad Pública (SSP) (similar to the U.S. Department of Justice) and took over investigative capabilities that previously resided with the Agencia Federal de Investigación (AFI, or Federal Investigation Agency). In 2010, there were efforts to consolidate state and municipal police forces into 32 state-level agencies. Although such consolidation can lead to improved coordination of resources and take advantage of economies of scale, thereby improving efficiency, it can also lead to the concentration of power into fewer hands and, potentially, to more corruption and abuse. Although we do not mean to suggest that such police force consolidation and reorganization should not take place in Mexico, it does suggest that care must be taken to ensure that reform does not lead to unintended adverse effects.

In the next section, we discuss specific key police reforms since the late 1990s. Excellent and more detailed history of police reform can be found in Sabet (2010a, 2010b) and E. Olson (2009).

Overview of Police Reforms

Mexico's police forces operate at the federal, state, and municipal levels. Although the police forces have complex and changing functions and jurisdictions, they are generally divided into crime prevention and crime investigation. There are currently two federal police forces (the PF and the Federal Ministerial Police [Policía Federal Ministerial, or PFM]), state police forces associated with each of the 31 states (plus two for the federal district in Mexico City), and a large number of municipal police forces. According to the June 2010 issue of *Justice in Mexico News Report*, there are about 2,022 municipal police departments, of which half have fewer than 20 police officers.

Of the 368,000 police officers in Mexico as of June 2007, only 6.5 percent are federal law enforcement officers (Lecuona, 2009). The PFP (the predecessor to the PF) employed most (76.5 percent) of these federal law enforcement officers, while the remainder were part of the PFM, the investigative forces. About half of police officers in Mexico are employed at the state level (32.6 percent of all officers) or by the federal district in Mexico City (20.9 percent), while 40 percent are employed at the municipal level.

Perhaps the one constant of policing in Mexico in the past two decades has been change. Police reform has been an ongoing, multidimensional effort to improve capacity and effectiveness. At the same time, there has been a similar reform of judicial institutions, and, although we focus on police reforms, it is clear that judicial reform affects the effectiveness of police reform and vice versa.

Much of the police reform effort has been concerned with modernizing and professionalizing the police forces, as we discuss in greater detail in the next section. These efforts include organizational restructuring, particularly at the federal level; expanding public security budgets; enacting new personnel management policies (e.g., selection, training, discipline, promotion, and compensation); enhancing operations through technology, equipment, doctrine, and communications; collecting data to permit oversight; and even militarizing the police by replacing police officers with military personnel. Some of these efforts have overlapped. For example, organizational restructuring has occurred in conjunction with personnel management changes.

Police Reforms at the Federal Level

One of the most significant police reforms at the federal level occurred in 2009; it is a recent example of a chain of reforms that has been occurring in the past 15 years. The 2009 reform created the PF force, under the purview of the SSP, a cabinet-level ministry. The PF included what was formerly the protective arm of the police at the federal level, what had been called the PFP, charged with preventing and combating crime. The PFP, in turn, had been created at the end of the Zedillo administration a decade earlier in 1999, in an effort to consolidate and streamline multiple different specialized police forces into one agency.

The creation of the PF in 2009 put more investigative capabilities into the SSP, and the PF now includes both preventive and investigative functions. According to Lyons (2009), the new PF is being modeled after the U.S. Federal Bureau of Investigation and other international agencies, with the goal of replacing military personnel on the frontlines of the drug war with PF agents.

Prior to the 2009 reform, investigative capability at the federal level resided primarily with the Office of the Attorney General, under the auspices of the AFI.[1] When AFI was created in 2001, some additional reforms were made to modernize and professionalize the agency, including new officer selection criteria, policies to emphasize education, training, merit-based promotion, higher salaries, and improved equipment and facilities. For example, AFI investigators were required to have a college degree (Sabet, 2010a, 2010b). However, as discussed in the June 2009 *Justice in Mexico News Report*, AFI fell under the cloud of corruption in 2005 with

---

[1]   AFI had been created during the Fox administration in 2001 and replaced an earlier organization, the PJF, which was considered plagued by corruption.

an announcement by the Office of the Attorney General that nearly 20 percent of AFI's officers were under investigation for involvement with organized crime.

Under the 2009 reform, agents of the new PF not only have greater powers to gather intelligence on, combat, and investigate organized crimes; they also face new personnel management policies that include stringent screening, higher pay, and an education requirement to have at least a college degree. New recruits must pass a lie-detector test and are tested for their susceptibility to bribes. Former AFI agents were given priority in the new agency if they could pass a drug test, psychological testing, a background check, financial disclosure, and other screens (Lyons, 2009; Justice in Mexico Project, 2009b). In addition, the size of the police force at the federal level has expanded, with 10,000 new officers hired since 2008 (Ellingwood, 2010).

As mentioned earlier, there are two federal police forces in Mexico: the PF and the PFM. When investigative functions were given to the PF as part of the 2009 reform, AFI essentially dissolved and was replaced by the PFM. The PFM is an investigative agency that resides within the Office of the Attorney General, as did AFI before it; both PF and the PFM have investigative authority.

Police Reforms at the State and Municipal Levels

Although reforms at the federal level have received considerable attention, the federal police constitute less than 10 percent of all police officers in Mexico. The remainder comprises state, federal district, and municipal police officers.

As described by Sabet (2010a), several types of federal-level initiatives targeted at the state and municipal levels are noteworthy. The first is the Public Security Support Fund (Fondo de Apoyos a la Seguridad Pública, or FASP), a federal matching fund program in which the federal government provides funding to states for public security if the states match a percentage of the funding and meet reporting requirements. According to Sabet (2010a), the fund has supported communications (such as an emergency call system), as well as national crime and police databases. A second notable initiative is a 2008 joint United States–Mexico cooperation agreement, called the Mérida Initiative, that provides U.S. funding to Mexico's law enforcement agencies (at the federal, state, and municipal levels) primarily in the form, initially, of military technology and hardware, such as Black Hawk helicopters. More recently, the Mérida Initiative has supported a pilot program to train and equip police officers and information sharing at the local level, such as in Ciudad Juárez and Chihuahua (Embassy of the United States, 2010). Other pilot programs have been under way. Sabet (2010a) describes the Planning and Police Control System pilot under the Fox administration to improve local-level operations and internal supervision, though it has not always been adequately funded.

Another federal initiative targeted at local law enforcement is Subsidio de Seguridad Pública Municipal, or Subsidy for Municipal Public Security (SUBSEMUN). This fund was created in 2008 by the federal government to supplement local budgets for efforts to modernize and professionalize municipal police forces. As described by the Justice in Mexico Project (2009a), SUBSEMUN provided more than Mex$3.5 billion to 150 local governments in 2008, increasing to Mex$4.1 billion (in nominal terms) in 2009. To receive funding, municipal police forces must develop an organizational structure similar to that of the PF and a personnel structure (13 officer ranks) to permit professional development. They must raise officer salaries; improve police facilities; implement personnel management changes, including criteria for selection, training, promotion, and discipline; and adopt a national police operations manual. SUBSEMUN funds are targeted at municipalities deemed the most dangerous in terms of having the highest crime rates.[2] According to Justice in Mexico Project (2009a), México (the state) has the most municipalities receiving funds, followed by the federal district and Veracruz.

In June 2010, Mexico's National Public Security Council approved the creation of 32 state police forces that would unify the municipal police forces in their respective states. This proposal has support from the head of the SSP, Genaro García Luna, and the state governors. The initiative is intended to improve communication between different levels of law enforcement and introduce better state oversight of municipal law enforcement. It is also intended to take advantage of economies of scale. About half of municipal law enforcement agencies have fewer than 20 officers, and 400 municipalities (approximately 16 percent) have no police force (Justice in Mexico Project, 2010c). Several states have expressed interest in piloting unified police forces, including Baja California, Durango, Chihuahua, and Veracruz (see "Mapa interactivo," 2010).

In addition to these federal initiatives, numerous reforms have been made at the municipal level in an effort to professionalize local police forces in terms of selection and recruitment, training, pay and benefits, and equipment. Sabet (2010b) reports results of four cases studies, for the police forces of Chihuahua (city), Hermosillo, Mexicali, and Tijuana, as well as the results of a survey of eight others. He finds that, although substantial progress has been made in these areas, challenges remain in each area. Furthermore, despite progress, corruption and lack of professionalism still remain ongoing problems in municipal police forces.

In the areas of selection and recruitment, Sabet finds that several of the surveyed police forces now require a high school degree, though most still require only a ninth-grade education. The percentage of police in the surveyed departments with a high school education or above varied from 28 percent in Mérida to just over half in Ahome.[3] Furthermore, more municipal police forces are screening applicants and have introduced psychological and drug tests, background checks, interviews, and lie-detector tests to ensure that high quality applicants are hired. These efforts have been aided by the federal government's effort to introduce a national database of police officers. Nonetheless, municipal departments have been challenged to maintain these selection criteria in the face of substantial growth in hiring in recent years. When departments have sought to increase the number of officers, selection criteria have often been waived or ignored, and hiring has emphasized the number over the quality of officers hired. Training has also improved, with more municipalities providing basic cadet training to new recruits, some providing in-service training to existing officers, and many lengthening training time. Nonetheless, Sabet reports that increases in the sizes of municipal police departments have come at the expense of shortened training time and reduce training. Furthermore, although progress has been made in providing training to existing officers, several

---

[2] In particular, the federal government uses an objective, quantitative formula based primarily on crime rates and municipal population to identify and allocate funds to eligible municipalities (Estados Unidos Mexicanos, 2008). The two municipalities with the highest score in each state are selected, followed by the highest-rated remaining municipalities.

[3] The reported percentage with high school education or above in the survey was also around 50 percent in Chihuahua City and Cuernavaca, but not all data were reported in the survey for these departments.

of the municipal police forces surveyed by Sabet reported that more senior police, those who joined the force before the creation of the police academy, have never been formally trained.

Past research on the U.S. military, discussed in the preceding chapter, provides evidence on the positive relationship between education and aptitude entry standards and subsequent performance. The armed services in the United States use standards to screen recruits, including education, aptitude, physical fitness, moral character, age, indebtedness, and citizenship status. Studies of the U.S. Army show that high school graduates are less likely to drop out and are more likely to fulfill their service obligation, generally ranging from two to four years, than those without a high school diploma (Buddin, 2005). Other studies show that higher-aptitude recruits perform better at hands-on military tasks (Project A, 1990; Mayberry and Carey, 1997; Sellman, 1997). Thus, available evidence, though not specifically for police officers or for Mexico, indicates that policies to improve selection and training in Mexico's municipal police departments are important steps in the right direction. Like Mexico's municipal police departments, the U.S. military also faces the problem of lower standards when more recruits are needed and the force is growing. The U.S. military will provide waivers to applicants who fail to meet some entry standards. For example, in some circumstances, the U.S. military will give applicants with a criminal record a waiver and permit them to enter the military. Research shows that recruits who receive waivers do not perform as well and, specifically, are more likely to leave the military (Asch, Heaton, et al., 2010). Nonetheless, the U.S. military permits their entry, but each service has a waiver determination process. The waiver guidelines generally involve reviewing the applicants' overall eligibility, usually by senior leaders, to determine the "riskiness" of allowing entry. The U.S. military example suggests a possible approach that Mexico's police forces might consider for minimizing the risks of granting waivers for less qualified applicants.

Pay and benefits are another area in which significant strides have been made at the municipal level. For example, Sabet reports that Tijuana salary levels more than doubled during the period 2004 to 2007. However, a challenge that municipal police departments face is limited municipal budgets to permit substantial growth in police pay. Police personnel costs are already a substantial portion of municipal budgets, and efforts to increase police pay compete with other priorities, including efforts to improve police equipment.

As described in the previous chapter, research on the U.S. military shows that higher pay increases the number and quality of recruits and increases their retention (Asch, Heaton, et al., 2010; Simon and Warner, 2007). Although similar evidence is needed in the context of Mexico's municipal police, the research on the U.S. military suggests that efforts to improve the pay of police officers is likely to have a salutary effect on recruitment and retention. The budget constraints that Mexico's municipalities face are similar to those faced by other public security forces in other countries and represent a real challenge to ensuring adequate resources for setting compensation. Research from the U.S. military shows that targeted pay raises (rather than across-the-board pay raises), as well as recruitment and retention bonuses, can be more cost-effective recruiting and retention tools (Asch and Hosek, 1999). Targeted pay raises are those targeted to specific groups, such as specific occupational areas or specific groups of employees (such as senior ranked ones). Although pay is the foundation of any compensation system, recruitment and retention bonuses can be flexibly targeted to particularly desirable applicants or crucial employees and are more cost-effective than pay raises that are given to all personnel. Accountability is, of course, crucial, and it is important that the criteria for receiving bonuses and targeted pays are based on the strategic goals of the organization, are easily verifiable, and are not based on favoritism.

Sabet finds that equipment has also improved in recent years, with greater investments at the municipal level in technology and modernization, including better dispatch systems, surveillance cameras, patrol cars, firearms, and Global Positioning System (GPS) units. Still, despite these investments in new technology, relatively little has been devoted to maintenance, as reported by Sabet. For example, patrol-car maintenance has fallen behind in some cases.

Municipalities have also benefited from participating in a U.S.-based accreditation program, the Commission on Accreditation for Law Enforcement Agencies (CALEA). CALEA recognizes and certifies police agencies that meet a specific set of standards. Several Mexican police departments have received CALEA certification, including Chihuahua City and Mexicali. CALEA provides guidelines for reform based on best practices for municipal departments and represents an important step toward reform at the municipal level in Mexico. Research from the personnel economics literature also points to the importance of sets of reforms, rather than "one-off" reforms. That is, the literature shows that packages of human resource reforms are more effective than individual ones adopted alone (Ichniowski, Shaw, and Prennushi, 1997).

Militarization of Public Security in Mexico

The military has played an increasing role in efforts to combat violence, drug trafficking, and organized crime in Mexico, often replacing federal and local police officers who proved corrupt. In the late 1990s, the Zedillo administration removed 700 PJF (the predecessor of the AFI) officers and replaced them with 1,000 military personnel. When the PFP was created in 1999, it was formed in part by drawing on military personnel (Sabet, 2010a). More recently, 2,000 military personnel were deployed to Ciudad Juárez in 2008, and another 5,000 were deployed in 2009 to combat lawlessness in that city (Justice in Mexico Project, 2009a). A key reason that military personnel were deployed to conduct police operations is the general perception that military personnel are less corrupt than civilian police in Mexico (Moloeznik, 2009), as seen in the data we present in Chapter Four.

In 2010, the Mexican Senate passed several laws to clarify the role of the military in public security operations (Justice in Mexico Project, 2010b). The laws stipulated reforms to the military code of justice to strengthen the punishments to military personnel for joining or aiding organized-crime cartels. To some degree, these reforms are a response to concerns that military personnel are becoming more corrupt as they gain more exposure to drug traffickers.

Summary and Conclusions

Efforts to reform Mexico's police have been ongoing for decades at various levels of government. Often, these reform efforts focus on removing and replacing police offices or leaders who are perceived to be corrupt or inefficient. In other cases, reform has involved wholesale revision of the national police organizations, including the creation, merger, or removal of different police administrative units. It appears that the government's belief is that there are structural problems that need to be corrected with major reforms and that incremental change is not effective. The challenge with this approach is that it creates a state of constant flux, with little continuity or emphasis on long-term change and reform that builds over time. The use of the military in policing is an example of (perhaps justifiably) looking to short-term solutions to combat rising problems, such as drug cartel–related violence. A challenge with these kinds of responses is that they might not address more fundamental institutional issues.

On the other hand, these macrolevel changes in Mexico clearly indicate a desire to change the institutional context in which police corruption occurs. The literature points to the desirability of constraints on political power, broad political constituencies, and limited economic rents. Efforts to consolidate police forces within states might work to enhance political power rather than constrain it.

CHAPTER FOUR

Empirical Data on Corruption and Inputs to Professionalism in the Mexican Security Services

This chapter assesses the current state of corruption in Mexico, focusing especially on corruption and bribery associated with the police and security forces. We also present data on trends in inputs to police professionalism over the past decade. Previous research has assessed corruption in Mexico (e.g., Morris, 2003) and qualitatively explored the role of corruption in the police (e.g., Sabet, 2009). However, there has been little quantitative empirical work that describes the prevalence and perceptions of corruption within the security forces. In part, this is due to lack of data. Corruption is inherently hard to measure, and subnational data on corruption are limited for most countries. Fortunately, several recent data sets for Mexico provide the opportunity to look at state-level measures of corruption over the past decade and, in particular, focus on metrics related to the police and other security forces. We begin by reviewing the available data sources. Next, we discuss the definition of corruption, the approaches used to measure it, and the limitations of those measures. We then turn to state and national trends. The second half of the chapter focuses on the empirical evidence that can be brought to bear on reform efforts. We review past findings on the effects of Mexico's police reform efforts on corruption and then present an analysis of household data to assess whether there is evidence to suggest increased professionalization in the Mexican police and security sector, in terms of such inputs as pay and education. We acknowledge that existing data cannot be used to determine whether previous reforms have been effective at reducing corruption or even whether improved professionalization has in fact reduced corruption, but it is possible to look at inputs to police professionalism that previous chapters suggest are important to long-term efforts at reducing corruption to see whether progress has been made in these efforts.

Data on Corruption and Demographics in Mexico

Microdata on corruption are generally limited; however, Mexico is unusual in that there have been concerted efforts to assess household perceptions and experiences with corruption in the context of public services and crime. For the analysis in this chapter, we draw on three main sources of data:

- Encuesta Nacional de Corrupción y Buen Gobierno (ENCBG, or National Survey on Corruption and Good Governance), produced by Transparencia Mexicana. There are four waves of this nationally representative household survey on corruption: 2001, 2003, 2005, and 2007.

- Encuesta Nacional Sobre Inseguridad (ENSI, or National Survey on Insecurity), produced by Instituto Ciudadano de Estudios Sobre la Inseguridad (ICESI, or Citizens' Institute for Studies on Insecurity) and Instituto Nacional de Estadística y Geografía (INEGI, or National Institute of Statistics and Geography). ENSI is a nationally representative household survey that focuses on crime and insecurity. We use the three most complete recent waves: 2005, 2008, and 2009.
- Encuesta Nacional de Ingresos y Gastos de los Hogares (ENIGH, or National Survey of Income and Household Expenditure), produced by INEGI. This large, nationally representative household survey collects basic demographic and economic data; we use the most recent six waves: 2000, 2002, 2004, 2005, 2006, and 2008.

The three data sets provide distinct but complementary repeated cross-sectional data that allow us to construct a rolling snapshot of corruption in Mexico over the past decade, at both the national and state levels. The individual level data cannot be matched, and none of the data sources can be used to form a panel. But each of the three data sets provides high quality microdata.

Defining and Measuring Corruption

There is no single, universally accepted definition of *corruption*, but a common definition of *public corruption* is the misuse of public office for private gain (e.g., Svensson, 2005). Andvig and Fjeldstad (2001) provide an extensive discussion of the definitions of *corruption* and reinforce the idea that "[c]orruption is the abuse of public power for private benefit (or profit)" (p. 6). At its basic level, *corruption* is defined as the private wealth-seeking (or utility-seeking) behavior of someone with public authority or duties. Such individuals are in positions that require that they operate in the public interest, but instead they pursue private interests.

Corruption can be defined in economic or social terms. *Economic corruption* includes bribery, embezzlement, extortion, and fraud. *Bribery* is a payment, usually to a state official, to allocate the resources of the state or otherwise distribute benefits in a way that favors the person or entity paying the bribe.[1] *Embezzlement* is the theft of state resources by public officials who are charged with administering or managing them. *Extortion* is money or resources extracted by public officials through coercion, such as the threat of violence, while *fraud* involves deception, such as the manipulation or distortion of information by public officials for private gain. In this report, we focus primarily on bribery, since, of the difficult-to-measure aspects of corruption, it is the one that research and policy organizations have made the most attempts to measure quantitatively.

Corruption is difficult to measure because, almost by definition, it is a secretive activity.[2] One approach is to measure corruption by the number of arrests or convictions for corrupt

---

[1]   In contrast to economic corruption, social-related corruption does not involve monetary transactions but instead relies on favoritism. An example is nepotism, in which public officials distribute public resources in favor of family members, though clearly favoritism can also include diverting resources to friends and associates. Another form of favoritism that is also related to economic corruption is clientelism, in which public officials distribute public resources or prevent violence to those who provide favors or contributions, even if those contributions are not structured as a pure quid pro quo.

[2]   For a more detailed discussion of the challenges with and options for measuring corruption, see June et al. (2008).

activities. Although such measures can demonstrate the existence of corruption, arrests and convictions will reflect both corruption and the enforcement efforts to mitigate it, producing biased estimates of the extent of corruption. Perhaps the most common method of measuring corruption is based on surveys of experts, households, or business enterprises about their perceptions of corruption and experiences with it in terms of paying bribes and other activities.

There are widely used measures of corruption that assess corruption perceptions at the cross-country level. These include Transparency International's (TI's) Corruption Perceptions Index (CPI); the Bribe Payers Index, also developed by TI; and the Worldwide Governance Indicators. Although these indices provide an attractive means of comparing corruption across countries and comparing corruption within a country over time, they are also subject to numerous criticisms (Arndt and Oman, 2006; Knack, 2007). Methodological concerns aside, these indices could be helpful for tracking broad trends in corruption across countries or over time, but they are of little use for more detailed, microscale policy analysis.[3]

We use household survey data on both corruption perceptions and corruption experiences, which have their own advantages and limitations. Household surveys, including the ENCBG, ask individuals about their experiences paying bribes, providing an empirical measure of corrupt activity and not just perceptions or beliefs. In the case of the ENCBG, households also provide information about the size of the bribes they pay and for what services. This allows one to construct narrow, quantitative measures of corruption prevalence and magnitude.

The drawbacks to household surveys are that they capture only certain types of corruption, and households' responses are subject to multiple, immeasurable biases. Corruption metrics constructed from household experiences best capture petty corruption, since households typically have little opportunity to participate in grand corruption. Household perceptions, on the other hand, can be used to measure either grand or petty corruption. Households can have intimate knowledge and experience with corruption that affects them personally, but they might not be in a good position to assess, for example, high-level corruption in government procurement or bribes paid to federal judges. In this way, perception data from household surveys might or might not be more accurate than data from expert assessments. Household survey data can also be biased if households systematically misreport their true bribery experiences, either intentionally or unintentionally. Because they are being asked about illegal activities, households might underreport the frequency of bribes they pay, their magnitude, or both.[4] Moreover, if police substitute across sources of illicit income, a low level of police bribery reported by households could misrepresent overall corruption levels if police, for example, extract more bribes from firms.[5]

---

[3] There is also a small but expanding literature on "forensic economics" that seeks creative, market-based measures of illegal acts. For example, Jacob and Levitt (2003) devise a method for detecting teacher cheating using patterns in test-score data, and DellaVigna and La Ferrara (2010) detect firms' illegal arms-trade activity by using data on stock prices and political events likely to increase (or decrease) demand for illegal arms. In the area of corruption, Khwaja and Mian (2005) find evidence of political corruption using loan data in Pakistan; Hsieh and Moretti (2006) find evidence of bribery in Iraqi oil sales using price variations; and McMillan and Zoido (2004) document high-level corruption in Peru using record of bribes paid by the president's chief of secret police.

[4] As long as biases are consistent across respondents, we can still compare relative incidence of bribery, e.g., between states. If biases vary across groups—for example, due to differing expectations of respondent anonymity and fear of reprisal—then such comparisons are less reliable.

[5] We thank one of our reviewers for making this point.

National Trends in Corruption Perceptions, Reported Bribery, and Police Corruption

We consider first the overall perception and prevalence of corruption in Mexico. According to TI's CPI, Mexico ranks 89th, tying with such countries as Rwanda and Morocco (TI, 2009). However, the CPI provides no information about actual bribes paid; it only captures national-level corruption perceptions. Household survey data can fill this gap. Using the ENCBG data, we find that, in 2001, approximately 2.1 percent of households surveyed reported paying a bribe to a public servant within the preceding three months (Table 4.1). Moreover, the percentage of households reporting having paid a bribe to a government official increased nearly 150 percent between 2001 and 2007. The average bribe paid in 2001 was Mex$523, and the average bribe paid in 2007 was Mex$734 (all values in 2008 Mexican pesos).

The national corruption ratings from TI and statistics from the ENCBG mask substantial variation at the subnational level. For example, in 2001, 4.8 percent of households in Durango reported paying a bribe to a public official, nearly as high as the national average six years later, while the rate of reported bribe paying in Michoacán in 2001 was only 0.2 percent. In 2007, however, the state of Colima had the lowest reported incidence of bribe paying (1.6 percent), nearly one-tenth the rate of bribe paying in Chihuahua (9.9 percent). We investigate state-level data in more detail later in this chapter.

We can break down bribe-paying activities further by focusing on specific public services related to security and police. The top rows in Table 4.1 show the unconditional percentage of people who reported paying a bribe to avoid military service, to pass items through customs or across a border, and to avoid a penalty or detention from a traffic agent. The frequency of bribe paying across activities differs dramatically, as do trends over time. The last rows in Table 4.1 show the rate of bribe paying only for households that reported that they attempted to acquire the public service. For example, of the households that engage in military-related transactions (obtaining a military record or avoiding military service), few report paying bribes. In contrast, households that access customs and border services or risk being detained or fined by a traffic police agent paid bribes 31.9 and 56.6 percent of the time in 2007, respectively. Rates of bribe paying in these two areas have either remained constant (customs) or increased slightly (transit) between 2001 and 2007.

The results in Table 4.1 suggest that, although overall corruption shows an upward trend, corruption for activities associated with the police or security services does not. Bribes paid to the general category *public servants* doubled between 2001 and 2007; in contrast, essentially the same percentage of households report paying bribes for specific security- and safety-related services, such as to the customs and border police or to avoid military service.[6] This result holds for both overall service-related bribe rates and for rates conditional on households that experience or acquire the service. In other words, relative to "baseline" bribe rates, bribes paid to the military and police appear to have declined over the survey period.[7]

The ENSI survey on crime and victimization focuses specifically on bribes paid to police, and the results are generally consistent with the findings shown in Table 4.1. In Table 4.2,

---

[6]   Bribes paid to transit police do show a slight upward trend post-2003.

[7]   There are other possible explanations. For example, households could be less willing to report bribes in these three security-related categories in 2007 than in 2001, making it appear as though bribe incidence has fallen. We have no evidence to support such a hypothesis, however.

Table 4.1
National Trends in Corruption, 2001–2007: Households Responding to Questions About Bribes Paid (2008 pesos)

	2001	2003	2005	2007
All households having paid a bribe in the past three months				
Percentage that paid a bribe to a public servant	2.2 [1.9, 2.4]	3.5 [3.2, 3.8]	4.3 [3.9, 4.6]	4.9 [4.6, 5.3]
Average bribe paid (Mex$)	523.12	535.04	784.20	734.52
Number of bribes paid in sample	261	437	576	687
Percentage that paid a bribe to obtain a military record or skip service	0.9	0.8	0.5	0.6
Percentage that paid a bribe to pass things through customs, police post, sentry box, or border	2.6	2.3	2.2	2.4
Percentage that paid a bribe to avoid being fined or detained by transit agent	4.3	4.3	4.5	5.2
Conditional on households attempting to acquire a given service				
Percentage that paid a bribe to obtain military record or skip service	3.1	2.7	2.4	1.9
Average bribe paid (Mex$)	459.93	554.68	500.85	404.21
Percentage that paid a bribe to pass things through customs, police post, sentry box, or border	31.3	28.2	33.9	31.9
Average bribe paid (Mex$)	965.99	1,158.13	1,121.80	1,211.88
Percentage that paid a bribe to avoid being fined or detained by transit agent	48.3	47.0	49.3	56.6
Average bribe paid (Mex$)	324.58	207.93	292.75	241.41

SOURCE: Authors' tabulations based on ENCBG surveys from 2001 to 2007.

NOTE: Bracketed numbers in the first row indicate the 95 percent confidence intervals. Average bribe paid does not include bribes larger than Mex$40,000, which were deemed to be outliers and affected mean bribe amounts substantially. For example, without excluding outliers, the average bribe paid in 2001 to avoid being fined or detained by a transit agent was Mex$917.40. Full details are available from the authors upon request.

we present data from a series of questions that ask households to report whether government authorities have ever asked the respondent to pay a bribe for a "solicited service or infraction." Notably, households report being asked to pay a bribe much more often by transit police than all other types of federal and local police forces. In 2009, 28.4 percent of households were asked to pay a bribe by transit police, up from 22.1 percent in 2005 and an order of magnitude higher than the number of households asked to pay a bribe by the federal investigative police. Because of the large sample size for the ENSI data, the changes in bribes requested are statistically significant across all types of police.[8] However, with the exception of the transit police, the percentage point changes are all relatively small, and, in the case of federal preventive police and state judicial police, bribes fell slightly between 2005 and 2009. This is generally consistent with the ENCBG data and suggests—assuming that overall bribe rates are rising—that bribes paid to most types of police have not kept pace with general corruption trends.

---

[8] Two-sample proportions tests for 2005 and 2009 are all significant at z < 0.01.

Table 4.2
Bribe-Request Rates for Police Forces (percentage of households)

Requesting Force	2005	2008	2009
Federal preventive police	4.8	2.8	4.5
Federal investigative police	1.5	1.6	2.1
State judicial or ministerial police	6.1	4.7	5.9
Municipal or local police	8.8	9.7	10.9
Transit police	22.1	21.4	28.4

SOURCE: Authors' tabulations based on national averages from ENSI surveys from 2005 to 2009.

NOTE: Rates are unconditional and do not reflect the percentage of households that interacted with the police.

The results in Table 4.2 should be interpreted with caution, however, especially compared with the bribe-paying rates from the ENCBG data shown in Table 4.1. First, the rates from ENSI shown in Table 4.2 are unconditional, so a lower rate for federal investigators or a higher rate for transit police could reflect less or more frequent interaction by households with these forces. Second, ENSI asks household whether the police force in question *solicited* the bribe; it would not necessarily capture bribes offered by households voluntarily. In contrast, the ENCBG asks households to report whether they "[had] to *give* a bribe" for a specific service, but households could interpret some unsolicited bribes as obligatory. Finally, bribe requests reported in ENSI might not reflect actual bribes paid, since, in some cases, households might have refused to pay a requested bribe. Finally, ENSI provides much greater detail about bribes paid to specific types of police, while the ENCBG focuses on specific services without regard to the party to which the bribe was paid. Nevertheless, the results from the two surveys are broadly consistent, with households in each survey reporting high rates of bribe paying to traffic police and generally high rates of bribe paying to police overall.

The rates at which households pay bribes for activities associated with the police and military, shown in Tables 4.1 and 4.2, are consistent with household perceptions of corruption and their level of trust in public institutions. Table 4.3 shows household corruption perceptions for 12 occupations, in addition to the respondent's assessment of his or her personal level of corruption. Corruption-perceptions ratings can range from 1 to 10, with higher values indicating more corruption. In both 2005 and 2007, respondents ranked the police second most corrupt among the surveyed professions, tied with representatives, following politicians, and just ahead of judges. In contrast, soldiers (assessed only in 2007) were rated among the least corrupt occupations; only teachers and priests were deemed less corrupt. The corruption ratings for all professions were relatively stable between 2005 and 2007. There is relatively little variation in corruption perceptions across states. For police corruption, the lowest rated state in 2007 had an average rating of 8.2, while the highest was 9.3.

ENCBG data shown in Table 4.3 are supported by similar perception-based questions from ENSI that assess trust in public and social institutions. ENSI asked households how much they trust the local police, federal police, and army (armed forces). In 2009, households reported, on average, that they trusted the army (mean = 3.00) more than the federal

Table 4.3
Corruption Perceptions by Occupation for 2005 and 2007

Occupation	2005		2007
	Perception	Standard Deviation	
Politician	8.9	[1.7]	8.9
Representative	8.7	[1.8]	8.7
Police	8.7	[1.8]	8.7
Judge	8.4	[2.0]	8.3
Union leader	8.0	[2.1]	8.0
Bureaucrat	7.7	[2.2]	7.5
Business owner	7.6	[2.2]	7.4
Merchant	6.8	[2.4]	6.7
Journalist	6.3	[2.5]	6.5
Soldier	—	—	5.8
Teacher	5.6	[2.7]	5.7
Priest	4.6	[3.0]	4.9
Self	3.4	[2.4]	3.3

SOURCE: Values are mean corruption perceptions from the ENCBG, ranging from 1 to 10, with higher values indicating more corruption.
NOTE: Perceptions about soldiers were not asked prior to 2007.

police (2.32), who were, in turn, reported to be more trustworthy than the local police (2.04).[9] Household trust in the federal and local police was essentially unchanged between 2008 and 2009, though there was a slight increase in trust for the army (2.82 in 2008). As with household perceptions of corruption, of the 12 institutions about which ENSI asked, only the church (3.35) was trusted by households more than the army.

Correlates of Corruption at the State Level

As we mentioned earlier, there is significant variation in corruption measures at the state level. Moreover, we can compare how corruption varies at the state level with other data that are of interest to policymakers. Table 4.4 presents state averages of corruption perceptions and bribes paid to public officials from the ENCBG, along with data on income, crime rates, and two measures of whether a state is a "border state." The first border state measure captures whether a state shares any part of its border with the United States, while the second measure identifies those states that border a major U.S. city.

There are few obvious patterns that emerge from the data. On closer inspection, however, there are important associations across these variables. Households in states that share a border with the United States tend to report paying bribes more often (7 percent versus 4 percent) and report being the victim of a crime more often (22 percent versus 17 percent) than nonborder

---

[9] Scale ranges from 1 to 4, with 4 being most trustworthy.

Table 4.4
State-Level Tabulations on Corruption, Income, and Crime

State	Perceptions of Police Corruption (rating)	Perceptions of Military Corruption (rating)	Bribe Rate (public, preceding 3 months)	Household Member Victim of a Crime (in preceding year)	U.S. Border State	State with Major U.S. City Adjacent
San Luis Potosí	9.2	6.7	3	14	No	No
Baja California Norte	9.0	5.7	6	24	Yes	Yes
Durango	9.0	6.0	3	16	No	No
Morelos	9.0	6.2	6	27	No	No
Nayarit	9.0	6.0	4	20	No	No
Tlaxcala	9.0	6.1	3	13	No	No
Baja California Sur	8.9	5.2	6	19	No	No
Sinaloa	8.9	6.3	6	16	No	No
México	8.8	6.7	8	28	No	No
Yucatán	8.8	6.2	2	12	No	No
Zacatecas	8.8	6.7	4	16	No	No
Campeche	8.7	4.6	4	16	No	No
Chihuahua	8.7	6.6	10	21	Yes	Yes
Michoacán	8.7	5.6	4	13	No	No
Oaxaca	8.7	5.4	3	11	No	No
Puebla	8.7	5.4	10	24	No	No
Aguascalientes	8.6	5.8	4	22	No	No
Coahuila	8.6	5.3	6	21	Yes	No
Guanajuato	8.6	6.4	5	20	No	No
Nuevo León	8.6	5.8	5	19	Yes	No
Sonora	8.6	6.3	7	25	Yes	No
Jalisco	8.5	6.1	4	15	No	No
Tabasco	8.5	5.3	5	21	No	No
Veracruz	8.5	5.5	4	15	No	No
Colima	8.4	4.9	2	14	No	No
Guerrero	8.4	5.3	3	15	No	No
Hidalgo	8.4	5.8	5	20	No	No
Tamaulipas	8.4	5.3	8	24	Yes	Yes
Querétaro	8.3	5.2	6	19	No	No
Quintana Roo	8.3	5.2	5	13	No	No

Table 4.4—Continued

State	Perceptions of Police Corruption (rating)	Perceptions of Military Corruption (rating)	Bribe Rate (public, preceding 3 months)	Household Member Victim of a Crime (in preceding year)	U.S. Border State	State with Major U.S. City Adjacent
Chiapas	8.2	5.7	2	11	No	No
Distrito Federal	—	—	—	—	—	—
National average	8.7	5.8	5	18	—	—

SOURCE: All data except border state indicators are from Transparencia Mexicana (2007). Border state indicators are based on authors' calculations.

NOTE: Bribe rate refers to the percentage of households that paid any bribe for a public service. We exclude state-level data from the federal district because they might not be comparable to other states.

states. The differences are similar for states that border a major U.S. city, although the overall rates of bribery and self-reported crime are higher. However, households in border states do not perceive that either the police or army is more corrupt than do households in nonborder states.

Although perceptions of police corruption are correlated with perceptions of military corruption (0.513, p < 0.05), neither perception measure is correlated with actual incidence of reported bribes.[10] As described earlier, perception data likely reflect households' beliefs about grand corruption; households could also be interpreting "the police" broadly and providing their views on officials across states and levels of government.[11] Another explanation is that bribery is only one dimension of corruption, and household perceptions could be based on nepotism or other types of favoritism.

There is a strong association between the incidence of bribes and the self-reported crime rate (0.806, p < 0.05); states that experience more corruption also experience more crime. In contrast, corruption-perceptions measures are uncorrelated with the crime rate. Although we cannot make causal inferences about these relationships, taken together, these results suggest that perception measures do not accurately reflect important corruption outcomes for the police, a finding that is consistent with recent research (Olken, 2009). Corruption-perceptions data are easier to collect than data on actual bribes paid, but police and policymakers in Mexico should interpret perception data with caution, especially when using those data to inform policy or assess the progress of reforms.

Summary of Recent Corruption Trends

The data on corruption in Mexico are mixed. On the one hand, households' perceptions of police corruption and experiences with police-related bribery have not changed appreciably from 2001 to 2007. At the same time, there is some evidence that the overall level of petty corruption—as measured by bribes paid to public servants—has risen. Although it is possible to interpret this result as positive, we note that our data do not suggest broader, absolute improvements in corruption in the Mexican police; moreover, it is possible that households

---

[10] All correlations are Spearman rank correlations using state-level data unless otherwise noted.

[11] One might be concerned that overall public service bribe rates are a noisy proxy for bribes paid to the police, and this could explain the lack of correlation with police corruption perceptions. When we compare police corruption perceptions with bribes specifically related to the traffic police (the best police-specific measure of bribery), we find a higher correlation (0.237) that is still not statistically significant (p = 0.192).

have become more reluctant over time to report bribery experiences with the police, thus biasing our results. Furthermore, despite the stability over time, police corruption is relatively high, as measured by two different data sources. In the next section, we look at evidence on the success of past police reforms and assess inputs to police professionalism, factors that are thought to be important for effective long-term reforms.

Literature on the Effects of Mexico's Police Reforms

That Mexico's police suffer from lack of professionalism and problems with corruption is well-known, and the government has implemented programs designed to improve professionalism, as described in Chapter Three. There is a small but growing number of studies that have tried to assess the underlying causes of corruption (and related outcomes) in the police and the effects of various reforms. Much of this work has drawn on qualitative methods or case studies, largely due to lack of high quality quantitative data on outcomes, though a few have made use of some of the data sources described earlier in this chapter. We review briefly previous reform analyses and then turn to indirect evidence from our empirical data on shifts in professionalism in the Mexican police.

Shelley (2001) reviews the early reform efforts by the Fox administration in the context of historical challenges to reducing corruption in Mexico. She identifies key constraints to effective policing, including a lack of continuity in police leadership positions, the limited role and capabilities of civil society (including the media), and systemic problems of "inadequate vetting, training, and salaries" (p. 220). In a recent study, Sabet (2010a) reviews reform efforts over the past three Mexican presidential administrations, and he concludes that results have been mixed. He notes that greater resources have been made available for police activities. Federal and state spending on policing have increased in recent years, and the federal government has increased law enforcement capacity three-fold since 2000.

At the same time, Sabet, like Shelley, notes a lack of continuity from one political administration to the next, which leads to inconsistent leaders, policies, and priorities. For example, he points out that reforms in the early 2000s that involved renaming police forces and buying new uniforms—actions designed to signal a new approach to policing—were largely superficial and had little impact on fundamental police professionalism. Similarly, Sabet argues that the lack of policy coordination across administrations leads to ineffective policies: Even if one political leader strengthens police recruiting practices, the next administration might increase recruiting dramatically and necessarily reduce the quality of recruits (p. 19, see also Sabet, 2009).

LaRose and Maddan (2009) survey a panel of criminologist experts on law enforcement in Mexico and conclude that the majority of police reforms in Mexico have had little effect on law enforcement and specifically on corruption. They argue that the police are "outgunned and often undermined by cartel money and political influence" (p. 11). Morris (2007) uses quantitative data, such as the TI data on corruption perceptions in Mexico, and also concludes that there is no clear and conclusive evidence of a decline in corruption in Mexico.

Mohar (2009) focuses on police reforms in the state of Querétaro and finds that numerous reforms have been achieved, including a tripling of police pay and increased educational requirements, but they have been piecemeal, and a more comprehensive approach is needed. Both E. Olson (2009) and Salgado (2009) emphasize the importance of reforms at the state and municipal levels. They argue that much of the reform efforts have targeted the federal level even though federal police are a small fraction of the total police capability in Mexico. Both also argue that more needs to be done to improve accountability through better information, especially on state and municipal police.

Empirical Evidence on Professionalism in Mexico: Analysis of Age, Education, and Pay Trends

Ideally, we would use microeconomic data on professionalism, crime, or corruption outcomes to measure the effect of changes in compensation incentives or recruiting and selection policies. Unfortunately, there is a paucity of publicly available microdata on police wages, qualifications, and outcomes. Furthermore, police reforms have occurred frequently and often with multiple reforms enacted simultaneously, thereby limiting our ability to identify the effects of specific reforms on corruption outcomes. Another option is to use macrodata—for example, at the state level—to estimate the effect that reforms have on average outcomes. Although the existing data sources on corruption in Mexico yield some of the better subnational data available, the data on police reforms are limited, and reform efforts are not generally amenable to standard evaluation methods. Moreover, incentive programs, especially those designed to increase resources for the police, are often implemented at a municipal level or for only one branch of the security forces, which requires detailed outcome information that is beyond the available data. In short, the outputs of Mexico's reforms cannot be assessed using existing publicly available empirical data sources, and such an assessment would require new data collection efforts.

We focus instead on metrics of inputs, including education and wages. Mexico's police reforms are, at least in part, designed to increase the quality of the workforce and provide higher compensation, and we can assess the extent to which these inputs have changed over the past decade, since some of the reform efforts to professionalize the Mexican police have focused on education and pay. More generally, we explore how the police and military compare with other, similar workers in Mexico along key input dimensions using household survey data from 2000 to 2008. The discussion begins with a description of the definition of variables we use in the ENIGH data. We described the ENIGH data earlier in this chapter. Next, we provide comparisons of the age, education, and earnings of those in the security forces relative to the rest of the Mexican workforce.

Data and Variable Definitions

We use occupational and demographic information from the 2000 and 2008 ENIGH data. The ENIGH classifies respondent occupations in two ways: la Clasificación Mexicana de Ocupaciones (CMO, or Mexican Classification of Occupations) and el Sistema de Clasificación Industrial de América del Norte (SCIAN, or North American Industry Classification System). We define *police* as those respondents whose CMO codes correspond to "Police and Transit Agents" (8301). *Military* includes respondents with CMO codes 8310–8312, which correspond to "Workers of the Air Force," "Workers of the Marines," and "Workers of the Army," respectively. All other occupations are categorized as *nonsecurity*. Finally, in our analyses, we also expand our definition of *security forces* to include all respondents with CMO codes beginning with 83 and classify these individuals under *protection and surveillance services: armed forces*. In addition to police, transit agents, and military personnel, this classification includes firefighters, detectives, guards, customs and migration personnel, and similar security-related unspecified occupations. This group serves as one of the comparison groups, allowing us to obtain a more complete picture of the broader security sector in Mexico.

Along the SCIAN classification dimension, we pay special attention to the public administration industry, codes 9312–9314, which correspond to "Federal Public Administration," "State Public Administration," and "Municipal Public Administration," respectively. Most respondents who reported being a police officer, transit agent (97.4 percent in 2008 and 95.3 percent in 2000), or military personnel (100.0 percent in 2008 and 91.2 percent in 2000) were classified under one of these SCIAN codes.[12] This sector serves as a proxy for public sector occupations and a comparison group for individuals in police and military positions.

Finally, our analyses in the remainder of this chapter focus only on males, for two reasons. Both 2000 and 2008 ENIGH data contain data only for male military personnel. Among respondents who listed police and transit agents as their occupation, approximately 12 and 10 percent, respectively, in each year were female. For comparison purposes, we restrict sex to males across the two occupations of interest because empirical research shows that the female labor supply differs from that of men and we are not able to control for the factors that affect differing labor supply between men and women (see, for example, Klerman and Leibowitz, 1999, and Altonji and Blank, 1999).

Age and Education

Recent police reforms in Mexico have focused on improving the quality of people selected for police service, as described in Chapter Three. Multiple selection criteria and tests are being used, including drug testing, polygraphs, psychological profiling to identify propensity for corruption, and medical fitness. Another key criterion is education. Leaders of Mexico's security forces have placed a greater emphasis on recruiting high school graduates for protective services and college graduates for investigative services. Although age is not always a disqualifier for service, security-force manpower is generally relatively younger than the general population, for two reasons. In the case of military personnel, conscription of 18-year-olds in Mexico for one year of service means that much of the military will be young. In addition, security forces in general require "youth and vigor" because the work is active and can involve physical hardships. In the United States, security forces (e.g., the military and police forces) have age restrictions on who can be recruited, and retirement systems offer benefits at relatively young ages to induce people to leave before they are considered "too old" for service.

Age. Figures 4.1 and 4.2 compare the age distribution of security-force personnel with that of other groups, for 2000 and 2008, respectively, who are high school graduate males. We consider three groups of security-force personnel: police (all levels—federal, state, municipal), military, and the broader category of workers in protection and surveillance services in the armed forces. We compare the age distribution of these groups with the distribution for the male high school graduate (HSG) Mexican population that is part of the security (police or

---

[12] Compared with 2008 data, the 2000 ENIGH data are not as detailed in terms of SCIAN classifications. Specifically, only the first three digits of the SCIAN code are provided. However, we know from the 2008 codebook that SCIAN codes 561x range from 5611 through 5616, and codes 931x range from 9311 through 9319. Therefore, it is possible that some police, transit agents, and military personnel could belong to a SCIAN classification other than the four (5614, 9312, 9313, 9314) selected for analysis, but we cannot tell from the data. Therefore, the shares reported for 2000 are estimations.

Figure 4.1
Age Distribution of Security Forces Versus Nonsecurity Mexican Population Who Are Male High School Graduates, 2000

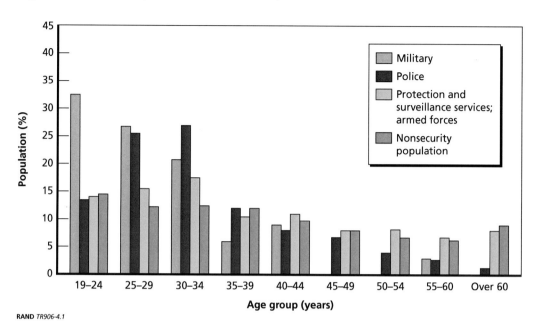

RAND *TR906-4.1*

Figure 4.2
Age Distribution of Security Forces Versus Nonsecurity Mexican Population Who Are Male High School Graduates, 2008

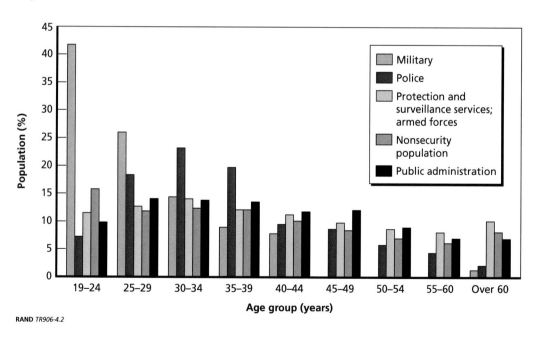

RAND *TR906-4.2*

military) forces. In 2008, we also compare these groups with those who work in municipal, state, or federal public administration, our proxy for public sector workers.

Figures 4.1 and 4.2 show that military personnel are substantially younger than both the overall Mexican male HSG population and police personnel and that the average age of military personnel fell between 2000 and 2008. In 2000, 32 percent of military personnel were between the ages of 19 and 24. By 2000, this percentage rose to 42 percent. Police personnel are also young relative to the general male HSG population, though not as young as military personnel. In 2000, just over half (52 percent) of police were between the ages of 25 and 34. Only 13 percent were in the youngest group, ages 19–24. Over time, police have gotten older. In 2008, only 42 percent of police were between the ages of 25 and 34, but 62 percent were between the ages of 25 and 39. Interestingly, the age distribution of those in protection and surveillance services in the armed forces is quite similar to the non–security-sector population in both 2000 and 2008. Similarly, those who stated that they worked in public administration in 2008 also have an age distribution that is similar to the non–security-sector male HSG population, though slightly more concentrated in the ages of 25–60.

The age-distribution comparisons suggest that both military and police personnel reflect a "youth and vigor" manning approach, with the military even younger than police personnel. Over time, police personnel have gotten older, on average. Unfortunately, we do not know the extent to which the observed age distribution reflects recruiting practices or retention behavior. In a push to expand their size in recent years, police forces might have more actively recruited military or police veterans who are older. Alternatively, reform efforts might have been successful in inducing midlevel police personnel to stay longer than in the past. More information is needed.

The age distribution of those who work in protection and surveillance services is quite similar to that of the nonsecurity population. This could reflect the possibility that this group includes people who are not directly involved in traditional police work but are administrators, secretarial staff, janitors and those who maintain facilities, and the like. If so, it is not surprising that the age distribution of this group is similar to that of the nonsecurity population. However, we do not have more detailed information on the composition of this group.

Education. Police reforms have included the requirement to increase the quality of those recruited, especially their educational attainment. Although some municipal police forces still require only a secondary education, many, such as the PF, also require a high school credential. We investigated changes in police education levels over time using the ENIGH data by tabulating the percentage of military and police personnel who had at least a high school credential in 2000 and 2008. We compare these tabulations with those for the nonsecurity male population in Mexico; the results are shown in Table 4.5.[13]

The table shows that military and police personnel are better educated than the nonsecurity male population, ages 18–60, in 2008, a significant change from 2000. Furthermore, educational attainment remained stable in Mexico between 2000 and 2008 but increased for military and police personnel considerably. The percentage of the male population, ages 18–60, that graduated from high school rose only marginally (from 19 percent to 20 percent) over this eight-year period, but it doubled for those who are either police or in the military from 12 percent to 24 percent and 12 percent to 25 percent, respectively. These tabulations suggest that, although the education level of Mexico's workforce has not changed appreciably, the education level of Mexico's security forces has improved (in terms of the percentage of the workforce with

---

[13] We also considered evaluating how educational attachment changed for age subgroups to see whether there is evidence of cohort effects (e.g., higher educational attachment for young, newly hired officers). Although the data suggest that education increases occurred across all age groups, the cell sizes for many age categories were too small to allow for valid comparisons.

Table 4.5
Percentage of Male Mexican Security-Force Personnel with at Least High School Education, Ages 18–60, by Year

Security Sector	2000	2008
Police or transit agent	12	24
Military	12	25
Police or transit agent or military	12	24
Protection or vigilance services in the armed services	13	18
Nonsecurity male population, ages 18–60	19	20

SOURCE: Authors' tabulations using ENIGH data.

at least a high school education) to the point at which, for 2008, we find evidence that they selectively recruit better-educated people relative to the general workforce.

However, it is unclear the extent to which this increase is due to the police reforms that occurred between 2000 and 2008 or whether the increase has helped mitigate corruption. It is also unclear whether the improvement occurred at all levels of policing: federal, state, and municipal. As discussed in Chapter Three, Sabet (2010b) surveys a selected group of 11 municipal police departments and finds that, for nine of the 11 departments, less than half their force had graduated high school. This is consistent with our data, but Sabet's sample is likely not representative of most municipal police forces in Mexico. However, it is possible that much of the increase observed between 2000 and 2008 occurred at the federal or state level, rather than the municipal level, and that the municipalities Sabet surveyed are unusual. Thus, although educational attainment for security forces between 2000 and 2008 has increased, the available data cannot tell us whether the increase is uniform across police forces in Mexico. Nevertheless, the data on education are consistent with the stated goals of Mexico's police reform efforts to professionalize police.

Comparisons of Pay for Security-Sector Versus Non–Security-Sector Personnel

From a personnel management perspective, a key role of pay is to enable the security forces in Mexico to attract and retain high caliber people who are honest and not corrupt. To do so, police and military personnel compensation must be competitive with civilian alternatives.

To be competitive, police and military pay does not necessarily have to be equal to civilian pay. When individuals assess the value of a career with the police force relative to other pursuits, they consider several factors. First, they consider compensation over the entire career, not just at a point in time. For example, entry pay might exceed the pay of other opportunities but might not rise very fast in the future. Second, they consider other financial benefits, such as speed of promotion, pension benefits, bonuses, and even bribes and other revenue-generating corruption opportunities, if available. Third, they consider nonmonetary aspects of a security-sector career. These can include training opportunities, as well as qualitative factors, such as whether the work is dangerous, requires specialized skills, occurs in desirable undesirable locations, or involves hardships. Furthermore, the next-best civilian opportunity might not involve working for money in a nonsecurity job but could involve attending college or working at home. However, in what follows, we measure civilian opportunities in terms of pay; since we cannot measure other job benefits, results should be interpreted with care.

Because there are many factors that affect the value of a job with the police, the pay levels that are adequate to attract and retain high quality people could be less than, equal to, or higher than pay for people with similar qualifications in the nonsecurity sector. For example, if the nonsecurity sector offers more training, better benefits, better career opportunities, and more desirable or less dangerous jobs are in terms of qualitative characteristics, then police and military pay must exceed that of the nonsecurity sector to attract and retain high quality people.[14] Similarly, if nonsecurity sectors are less desirable, then police and military pay could actually fall below the pay of non–security-sector jobs and still attract and retain high quality personnel.

On the other hand, the literature on corruption suggests that, in the presence of bribes and other financial returns to corruption, paying higher wages to potentially corruptible officials than to non–security-sector workers could induce police officers to forgo these bribe-taking opportunities. Thus, even if other factors lead to the conclusion that security-sector pay should be equal to or even less than nonsecurity pay, corruption opportunities could offset this effect and necessitate higher pay for security forces. We note that this mechanism is effective only to the extent that job-loss penalties for corruption are enforced. For this reason, the wage gap between security- and non–security-sector wages could provide some information about the opportunities for corruption, and a reduction in that gap is consistent with more competitive wages in the security sector and reduced incentives for corruption, all else equal. This subsection examines evidence on security-sector pay relative to pay provided in alternative jobs.

Table 4.6 provides pay comparisons of security- and non–security-sector personnel in 2000 and 2008 at each quartile of the pay distribution in each sector, where *pay* is defined as the monthly salary income from the respondent's primary job in real 2008 pesos. We limit the comparisons to males ages 18–60 because they have a stronger attachment to the labor force and are more likely to work full time and for a full year. For the nonsecurity sector, we also limit the population to those with high school certification because this is the stated benchmark for personnel quality in the security forces.[15]

Several findings emerge from Table 4.6. First, median pay (the 50th percentile) in the security sector was lower than median pay in the nonsecurity population in 2000 but roughly equal in 2008. Median monthly pay for police and transit agents in 2000 was about Mex$4,110, more than 35 percent lower than the median pay in 2000 for the nonsecurity population of about Mex$6,217. In contrast, in 2008, median pay amounts for the police and nonsecurity population were Mex$6,217 and Mex$6,431, respectively. The results are qualitatively similar for military personnel, although, in 2000, military pay exceeded police pay (both still fell short of non–security-sector pay).

Second, relative to non–security-sector pay, the structure of security-sector pay changed over time between 2000 and 2008. In 2000, the pay of police and transit agents fell short of nonsecurity pay at all quartiles, the 25th, 50th, 75th, and 99th. Falling short at the 99th percentile is not surprising because nonsecurity pay covers the private sector, including the top earners in Mexican society, thereby driving up the top 1 percent of the income distribution.

---

[14] As stated, we lack data on nonwage compensation and thus state unequivocally that police are compensated at lower rates than nonsecurity workers. However, Sabet (2010b) provides some limited evidence that many police forces pay salaries that are thought to be too low and offer little to no benefits.

[15] To facilitate comparisons between 2000 and 2008, we apply this benchmark to both years, though it might be more relevant in 2008 than in 2000 given the history of police reforms (see Chapter Three).

Table 4.6
Percentiles in 2000 and 2008 of Mexican Police Pay and the Pay of the Nonsecurity Male Mexican Population Ages 18–60 with High School Education (monthly salary in 2008 pesos)

| | | | Pay at Each Percentile | | | | | | | |
| | N | | 25th | | 50th | | 75th | | 99th | |
Population	2000	2008	2000	2008	2000	2008	2000	2008	2000	2008
Police and transit agents	74	263	3,580	4,697	4,110	6,217	5,132	8,301	12,171	24,932
Military	33	76	4,416	5,195	5,045	6,326	5,860	7,332	26,787	14,038
Nonsecurity population	1,529	7,542	3,772	3,831	6,487	6,431	10,769	11,013	49,117	47,049

SOURCE: Authors' tabulations using ENIGH data.

Unlike pay in the nonsecurity sector, security-sector pay includes only the public sector. However, for the other percentiles, these comparisons indicate that police pay in 2000 was less competitive than nonsecurity pay.

We see a similar pattern for military pay in 2000, with the one difference being that pay at the bottom quartile is actually higher for military than for non–security-sector personnel. It is possible that those at the bottom quartile are entry personnel, and military pay might have been higher for entrants in an effort to attract high quality people into the military in 2000.

In contrast, in 2008, the pay for police and transit agents exceeded non–security-sector pay at the first quartile (Mex$4,697 for the latter and Mex$3,831 for the former), was roughly the same at the second quartile (Mex$6,217 versus Mex$6,431), and fell short at the top two quartiles. These comparisons are consistent with police reform efforts to increase pay at the lower levels, probably for entry-level and less experienced police who generally receive lower pay, but not at the higher pay levels, most likely people who are more senior. Put another way, the data suggest that the security sector became significantly more competitive with the non-security sector for those in the bottom half of the pay distribution, with the incentives for corruption (as measured by the gap in pay) narrowing. However, pay still fell short relative to the nonsecurity sector for higher-paid security personnel in the top half of the distribution. These results are suggestive rather than definitive because the comparisons control only for gender, education, and broad age ranges and do not control for other factors that might have changed over time. For example, as shown Figures 4.1 and 4.2, police got somewhat older, so the increase in pay in Table 4.6 could reflect the higher pay associated with more senior police personnel. On the other hand, Figures 4.1 and 4.2 also show that military personnel got younger, yet we observe similar increases in pay in Table 4.6 for military as for police personnel.

The differences by percentile in Table 4.6 suggest that pay comparisons might differ at different stages of an individual's career (entry-level versus more senior personnel). We investigate how the structure of security-sector pay across age groups compares with pay structure in the nonsecurity sector in Figures 4.3 and 4.4. The figures show, for 2000 and 2008, respectively, how median pay varies by age group for police and military personnel in each year. To aid comparisons, the figures also show the percentiles of monthly pay in the nonsecurity sector for male HSGs. The profiles allow us to investigate whether pay in particular age groups for the police and military falls short or exceeds non–security-sector pay in those age groups and where in the distribution of nonsecurity pay median security-sector pay falls.

We note two important issues in interpreting the findings in these figures. First, the median of security-sector pay includes police, transit agents, and military personnel. Therefore, the figures cannot discern differences across these three groups. Second, pay differences across age groups can be interpreted as differences in pay over a career, but care must be taken in making this interpretation because the data we use are actually snapshots at two different points in time. Thus, the figures show pay at different ages among people who entered the police and military forces in different years, rather than pay at different ages among people who entered the security sector in the same year. Because people entering in different years might be subject to different labor market conditions or other "demand and supply" shocks over their career, and these shocks might differ for people in different occupations and entering cohorts, observed differences across occupation in wage–age profiles in cross-sectional data might not reflect actual differences in how pay grows over the career of individuals in different occupations. Tracking pay over individual careers for people who entered at the same time requires longitudinal microlevel data, information that is unavailable to us. Our approach therefore limits our ability to making inferences about true career–pay profiles.

Figure 4.3 shows that, in 2000, the median of security-sector pay did not vary with age in general (in 2008 pesos). Median pay jumps by Mex$3,000 for those ages 40–45, but, for those age 50 and older, median pay is the same as it is for those at the beginning of their career, about Mex$5,000 per month. This pattern is in striking contrast with pay in the civilian nonsecurity sector. In the nonsecurity sector, median pay is greater for those at older ages, though it drops for those ages 55–60.

Theoretically, we expect pay to be greater at older ages for two reasons. First, the academic literature consistently finds that pay grows with job experience, reflecting the accumulation and the returns to general human capital over the career. As workers gain job and labor market experience, their pay grows because they are more productive both in their current job and in other jobs. Furthermore, early in their careers, workers invest in education and other forms of formal general human capital or skill development, reducing their initial pay but resulting in higher pay later in their career. Second, theories of incentives, such as those discussed in Chapter Two, suggest that pay rises over the career to induce higher productivity among junior workers. In the case of the public sector, pay raises over the career generally come in the form of promotion to higher ranks that offer higher pay. However, we cannot infer whether there is support for either explanation in the tabulations in Figure 4.3, because we are comparing pay by age across different people at a point in time, rather than comparing pay by age for the same individuals over time.

Nonetheless, the tabulations are consistent with both explanations for why pay rises at older ages. The virtually flat pay profile for security-sector personnel in 2000 is consistent with little or no incentive to invest in or accumulate general human capital and no pay incentives for higher productivity, in contrast with the nonsecurity sector, in which median pay is greater at older ages. Furthermore, consistently with the findings in Table 4.6, median security-sector pay falls far short of civilian non–security-sector pay, except at entry (ages 18–24). At entry, median security-sector pay lies at the 60th percentile of the pay of male HSGs in the nonsecurity sector, though the results in Table 4.6 suggest that this is probably driven by the pay of military rather than of police and transit agents. By ages 25–29, median security-sector pay lies at the 50th percentile, and, by ages 45–49, it lies at or below the 20th percentile. Thus, although the security-sector profile is flat, relative to the nonsecurity sector, the profile actually declines across age groups, from the 60th percentile for junior personnel to the 20th percentile

Figure 4.3
Percentiles in 2000 of Mexican Non–Security-Sector Pay for Male High School Graduates, and Median Security-Sector Pay, by Age (monthly salaries in 2008 pesos)

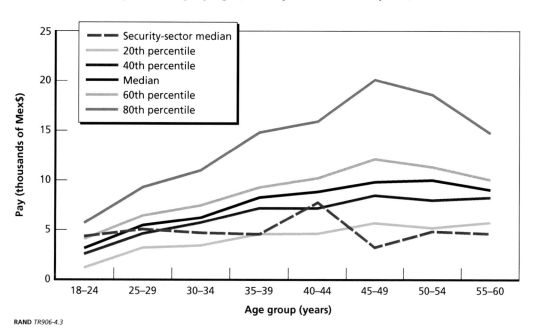

for senior personnel. The comparison shows that relative pay fell far short for senior security-sector personnel in 2000.

It is important to note that our metric of pay does not include bribes and other financial returns to police corruption. Given the large "pay gap" for senior security-sector personnel in 2000, the question of why senior police personnel would stay in the police force in 2000 arises. One possible reason is that corruption opportunities were greater for senior personnel because they had an entire career to develop corruption networks and reap the returns. Thus, for senior personnel, a larger share of their total income could have come from corruption activities. Importantly, we have no direct evidence of this effect. Figure 4.3 suggests that the pay for senior police and military personnel fell short of non–security-sector wages, consistent with fewer incentives to invest in skills, be productive, and avoid corruption. We reiterate that the result is suggestive because we do not actually track pay by age over the career of individual police officers.

Figure 4.4 shows a different pattern for 2008. The median for security-sector pay in 2008 was flat across age groups until age 40; median pay is higher for those over 40, until the age group 55 to 60. Thus, unlike in 2000, pay is greater for more senior military personnel, police, and transit agents in 2008. Furthermore, pay differences between those in their midcareer (between the age groups 35–39 and 45–49) and junior personnel are greater for security forces than for nonsecurity personnel, though differences are smaller thereafter. Like in 2000, pay at the entry ages in 2008 is high relative to non–security-sector pay. For example, at ages 18–24, median pay of security personnel is above the 80th percentile of male HSGs in the nonsecurity sector. It remains above or at the 50th percentile for those in age groups 25–29 and 30–34. For those in age groups above age 35 and until ages 55–60, median pay for security forces is around the 40th percentile of civilian pay or even higher. Like in 2000, median pay of security personnel across age groups is generally flat relative to non–security-sector pay, at least for those

Figure 4.4
Percentiles in 2008 of Mexican Non–Security-Sector Pay for Male High School Graduates, and Median Security-Sector Pay, by Age (monthly salaries in 2008 pesos)

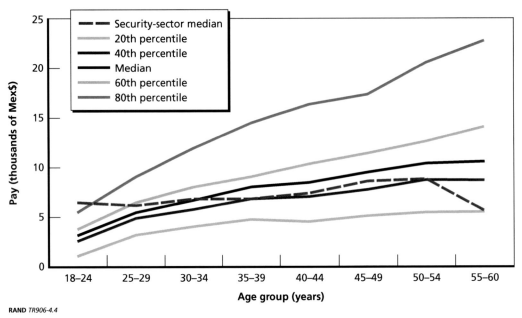

RAND *TR906-4.4*

less than age 55, but, unlike in 2000, the pay levels for security personnel in 2008 are substantially higher. For those ages 55–60, security-sector pay is lower, suggesting a strong incentive to induce the most-senior people to leave.

The results in Figure 4.4 indicate that median pay fell short of civilian non–security-sector pay among more senior personnel over age 35, but the "pay gap" is smaller in 2008 than 2000. Assuming that the characteristics of being a police officer did not change significantly between 2000 and 2008, the data are consistent with a reduced incentive to engage in corruption, relative to 2000, for many segments of the age distribution. Similarly, unlike in 2000, we observe higher pay between the age groups of 35–39 and 50–54 relative to the pay of more junior personnel, consistent with providing greater incentives to invest in human capital and be productive. Again, pay differences by age relative to the civilian sector might be too little to provide meaningful incentives. We also emphasize that these are cross-sectional comparisons and might reflect cohort effects, so our conclusions could be driven by other effects at play.

What Can We Learn?

Households in Mexico are concerned about corruption and assess the level of corruption in the police as high. Although trust in the armed forces is higher than trust in most occupations—and perceived levels of corruption lower—the police garner significantly less trust at all levels of government. Reports of bribes paid for services associated with the police, however, tell a more subtle story. Relative to overall levels of bribery to public servants, which have been increasing, experiences with police corruption (actual bribes paid) have been relatively flat, as we show in this chapter using two independent, nationally representative surveys. Moreover, corruption perceptions and corruption experiences are generally not correlated, suggesting that households might be assessing the level of corruption in their state on something other than the bribes they pay on average. These data should be interpreted with caution, but they are consistent with a situation in Mexico in which anticorruption efforts are having some effect in stemming the relative growth of police corruption, and household perceptions are not consistent with actual incidence of bribes.

Data on inputs to professionalism (education and wages) are also broadly consistent with efforts to reform the police. Comparisons between security-sector and non–security-sector pay in 2000 and 2008 suggest substantial improvement in 2008. Security-sector pay levels in 2008 are higher than both levels in 2000 and non–security-sector pay in 2008. Although, in both time periods, security-sector pay is generally flat across age groups relative to non–security-sector pay, the absolute level of pay increases is greater for older personnel after age 35 in the security sector in 2008, unlike in 2000. However, pay still falls short for more senior personnel, suggesting the possibility of adverse retention incentives and inadequate incentives to develop skills over the career, be productive, and avoid corruption.

Unfortunately, for the reasons discussed at the beginning of this chapter, we are unable to identify the degree to which improvements in police, military, and transit agent pay in 2008 relative to that in 2000 are due to specific police reforms. It is likely that such improvements would not have occurred without police reform, but we have no information about which reforms, other than general pay raises, were effective and why or whether these improvements have in fact led to less corruption. Better data and additional analysis is required to address these questions, a topic we discuss further in the final chapter.

We note, however, that although police salaries appear to have increased on average, there might be reasons that we do not see a concomitant fall in the absolute level of corruption over the same time period. First and most obviously, reforms take time. Some major reforms (e.g., SUBSEMUN) are only just being implemented, and these programs, along with general wage increases, are not designed in such a way as to immediately reduce corruption levels.

There is also that concern that pay raises alone are not enough to reduce corruption. As the theoretical literature on compensation and bribery makes clear, pay increases without credible enforcement are unlikely to reduce bribery rates. Unfortunately, there are few data regarding enforcement rates in Mexico's police departments. Moreover, reports of wholesale firings, such as the dismissal of 3,200 federal police who failed lie-detector tests or other anti-corruption checks earlier this year (A. Olson, 2010), are not encouraging. It is doubtful that large-scale layoffs are due to selective enforcement of rules against corruption; rather, they are more likely the result of screening criteria that are applied with a broad brush.[16] This could undermine enforcement expectations, causing police to assume that firings are not tied to their actual behavior. Moreover, to maintain staffing levels, these departments will need to hire hundreds of new workers quickly, which could result in low quality hires if departments do not have adequate hiring mechanisms in place or if rapid hiring puts undue strain on systems designed to produce high quality recruits.

---

[16] See similar accounts in Tlalnepantla (Justice in Mexico Project, 2009a) and Monterrey (Justice in Mexico Project, 2010c), in which municipal police departments each fired (or asked for voluntary resignations of) more than 100 workers simultaneously. In Monterrey, this constituted 40 percent of the workforce.

CHAPTER FIVE

Conclusions

This report considers the problem of corruption in the Mexican police and security forces through the lens of economic incentives. Specifically, we address the questions of what the institutional and incentive roots of corruption are; what the policies are that are understood in the literature to be effective in mitigating corruption, focusing on compensation and personnel policies; and what evidence is available to suggest that these policies might be effective, both in general and in the context of corruption among Mexico's security forces. We summarize our main conclusions in this chapter and discuss next steps in terms of data and research.

The main conclusion is that we find some evidence that Mexico is making positive progress in its efforts to reform its security forces based on the literature and the limited evidence we were able to access, but the scant evidence available on effectiveness suggests that much more effort is needed. Part of the additional effort should come in the form of improved auditing, including better data collection, and evidence-based policy that is informed by research and analysis. We elaborate on these themes in the remainder of this chapter.

Some Evidence of Progress

We began our analysis with a review of the theoretical literature on the role that institutions and incentives have in corruption. Weak economic institutions, such as the lack of property rights and free markets, are a critical determinant of corruption when groups that hold power also influence the choice of economic institutions. Stronger economic institutions are more likely to be found when there are constraints on political power, when power is shared across a broad base of people, and when opportunities for corruption are limited because of limited economic rents.

In the context of Mexico, this literature suggests that the numerous reforms that Mexico has undertaken to improve its judicial system and police forces are ones that the literature identifies as the right types of policies to potentially strengthen economic institutions, though we have no evidence on the actual effects of these reforms. On the other hand, the rising drug trade since the 1990s has been a destabilizing factor for Mexico and presents huge opportunities for corrupt officials to extract economic rents. Furthermore, efforts to consolidate the various police forces in Mexico at the federal and state levels could, on the one hand, help these forces improve coordination and take advantage of economies of scale, but, on the other hand, they could reduce the political power base and increase corruption. Empirical evidence is mixed on the effects that centralization has on corruption. Still, the move toward greater consolidation should be viewed with caution. In short, from an institutional perspective, Mexico is making progress in terms of greater political turnover and by adopting policies to strengthen institutions, but the effects of these policies are unknown, and, importantly, the drug trade represents an enormous challenge to these institutions.

The power of incentives in improving performance, including reducing corruption, rests on strong institutions. For corruption-reducing incentives for law enforcement officers to be meaningful, the "principal" in the "principal–agent" relationship (namely, political and law enforcement leaders) must themselves be honest and work in the public interest. Given an honest principal, the incentive literature, in the context of the public sector, points to the effectiveness of promotion schemes, higher pay, pay that varies over the career, and entry standards as mechanisms to increase productivity and induce honesty.

This finding suggests that the types of reforms recently undertaken by Mexico to professionalize its police forces through compensation and personnel management policies are on the right track and represent progress, though again we reiterate that we have no evidence that such progress has indeed resulted in less corruption. On the other hand, the literature points to the importance of getting the specific details of these programs right. Promotion must be merit based and not subject to favoritism, lobbying, and other influence activities, and the pay structure associated with promotion should be skewed (i.e., rising pay increases with rising rank). Pay over the course of a career, and not just entry pay, must be structured to ensure that the value of joining, as well as staying, in the police force exceeds the value of alternative employment. Rising pay over the career also rewards human-capital development and provides better productivity incentives. Furthermore, efficiency-wage programs that pay officers more than the next-best employment alternative can be effective in mitigating bribe-taking only if they are supported by effective enforcement and firing for those caught taking bribes. Thus, to effectively professionalize law enforcement officers, it is not sufficient to merely raise entry pay or define a promotion scheme.

We also examined available empirical data to describe the current state of police corruption in Mexico. We found that, although household perceptions of police corruption and experiences with police-related bribery did not change appreciably between 2001 and 2007, there is some evidence that the overall level of petty corruption—as measured by bribes to public servants—has risen. On other hand, with the exception of the transit police, security-related bribery has been relatively stable, compared with bribes to public servants in general. Bribe rates to public servants doubled between 2001 and 2007, with the average amount of the bribe increasing by approximately 40 percent. In contrast, reported bribe-paying for services related to the military and customs and border police was relatively stable. In the case of transit police, we find some evidence that the percentage of households paying has increased slightly since 2003. Our analysis of requests for bribes by federal, state, and municipal police showed a similar pattern. These results indicate that, although corruption among Mexico's military personnel and customs and border police has not declined in absolute terms, it has declined relative to the overall trend in corruption among public servants in Mexico. Although it is possible to interpret this result as positive, we note that our data do not suggest broader, absolute improvements in corruption in the Mexican police; moreover, it is possible that households have become more reluctant, over time, to report bribery experiences with the police, thus biasing our results. Finally, it is important to note that, despite the stability over time for some parts of Mexico's security forces, police corruption, as measured by two different data sources, is also deemed to be relatively high. Thus, although there is some evidence to suggest progress, it should be interpreted with caution.

We also considered evidence on recent changes in the age, education, and pay of security-force personnel in Mexico using household data, since these metrics are related to the recent Mexican police reforms. In 2008, police were better educated than the non–security-sector workforce, representing an improvement over 2000, when they were less educated. In 2008, the median pay of police also exceeds the median pay of males in the civilian nonsecurity workforce who graduated high school. Again, this represents an improvement, since median pay of police lagged behind that of their civilian counterparts in 2000. Though there are important drawbacks of using pay comparisons to make inferences about the competitiveness of law enforcement, our pay comparisons suggest that police pay was more competitive in 2008 than in 2000 and that the incentives for corruption were reduced, all else equal. That said, it is unclear that the higher pay levels in 2008 were sufficient to prevent (or reduce) actual corruption and bribe-taking. In addition, in 2008, the pay of more senior law enforcement officers was lower than for the male HSG civilian workforce. Thus, broadly speaking, police pay has improved, but more needs to be done. Moreover, at this point, we have no evidence to identify the extent to which improvements are linked to changes in corruption.

In this report, we have not focused in detail on the relationship between police corruption and drug-related violence, and we have not attempted to assess how increases in cartel activity have affected police professionalism. However, there is an important intersection between violence and police pay that is worth noting. As outlined in Chapter Four, police compensation is a function of numerous factors, including training opportunities, pensions, and job risk. As cartel-related violence rises in some parts of Mexico, there will be increasing pressure on police wages as being employed as a police officer becomes riskier.[1] For a given wage, more violence directed at police—and thus a higher risk of injury or death—could increase the minimum wage that police recruits are willing to accept for a *given level of performance*.[2] In other words, if increasing wages leads to lower corruption, as predicted by theory, we would expect the corruption-reducing effects of higher wages to be offset when police face greater potential for injury or loss of life, since individuals will demand higher salaries simply to work in a higher-risk environment.[3] Under these conditions, salary increases might need to be higher than otherwise expected to deter corruption and encourage police to retain or accept jobs in more violent environments.

Next Steps

The literature on worker compensation is well developed, and economic theory suggests that worker pay can be an important tool in reducing corruption and bribe-taking. Empirical evi-

---

[1] An alternative interpretation is that the violence might deter police from interacting with cartels and thus reduce bribe-taking; however, previous research and anecdotal accounts (see Sabet, 2010a) suggest that police are typically unable to avoid interacting with cartels and often face a choice between taking bribes or suffering violent consequences.

[2] This will be true of the military, as well, to the extent that it is involved in risky cartel-related security activities. However, the relationship between job risk and compensation expectations for military personnel might not be the same as for the police.

[3] This also raises a subtle but important point. Raising salaries will deter police from taking bribes as long as getting caught carries the punishment of job loss. But when the police face the risk of death in their jobs (e.g., if they do not agree to act on behalf of a cartel instead of acting in the public interest), then their potential disutility (cost) from not cooperating with the cartel is beyond value. Increasing salaries alone will likely do little to offset this type of downside risk.

dence on the effectiveness of compensation and personnel management primarily comes from military manpower analyses in the United States. But there is little empirical evidence related to corruption and police reform to guide policymakers as they search for ways to use professionalism as a means to stem corruption in Mexico's law enforcement agencies. Data are limited, and anticorruption policies for the police have rarely been subjected to formal evaluation or even designed in such a way as to facilitate rigorous review. Evidence from case studies, correlations from aggregate data, and qualitative assessment are suggestive but not conclusive.

Unfortunately, the potential for and impact of reforms to reduce corruption in Mexico is no clearer. In Chapter Four, we reviewed rich household data on corruption in Mexico and examined key inputs to police quality, including education and wages. None of these data sets allows us to directly evaluate past reforms. Moreover, the lack of high quality, publicly available data on key issues, including police wages and training, crime, and public security budgets, limits more systematic analyses of Mexico's reforms, the type of analyses that guide effective, long-term reforms. We therefore consider a set of specific steps that policymakers and research communities could pursue to provide better data and inform evidence-based policy.

Developing Institutional Data and Analysis Capabilities

Numerous private and not-for-profit organizations in Mexico have brought to bear greater transparency on corruption and Mexico's law enforcement efforts by gathering and disseminating data and statistics related to corruption perceptions, crime rates, and the drug trade. Websites for such organizations as Transparencia Mexicana, the Center of Research for Development (CIDAC), Seguridad Pública en México, Latinobarómetro, and others provide excellent sources of information for researchers, policymakers, and the general public in Mexico on law enforcement efforts, crime, and corruption perceptions.

An important advantage of being able to access private (nongovernmental) sources of information about crime and corruption is that the sources themselves are less vulnerable to the influence of public sector corruption. However, a disadvantage is that private sources must rely on existing public administrative data sources that might be incomplete and inaccurate, or they must rely on surveys that are based on potentially imperfect respondent recall and sampling problems. Furthermore, different organizations focus on different topical areas, and, because the areas are not centrally coordinated, there can be important information gaps.

To improve completeness, accuracy, and ease of data availability on crime and corruption, a government-led coordinated effort is required to collect, audit, report, and maintain a historical inventory of comprehensive and detailed microlevel data on crime, corruption, and law enforcement on an ongoing basis. To minimize the influence of public sector corruption in the gathering and reporting of such data, it will be critical that an independent organization or agency, relying on independent experts, be given the mandate to audit data collection and management processes to ensure that organizations tasked with the various data-related efforts are accountable. Such an audit agency should provide publicly available, ongoing reports on the transparency, accuracy, and completeness of the data, as well as the ease of usability and accessibility.

As part of the effort to create data capacity on law enforcement, crime, and corruption, an independent government commission should be established. This commission should identify the types of data that should be collected, the information that should be gathered, what agencies should be responsible for collecting and maintaining data, and the sources of funding for data collection and maintenance. The commission should be composed of nationally recognized experts on law enforcement, statisticians, researchers, and representatives of the law enforcement community. Because data needs change over time, the commission should be convened at regular intervals, such as every four or five years.

To ensure that corruption-related police reforms in Mexico are based on sound evidence, it is also critical that Mexico develop a research capability to inform policy decisionmaking. The research capability could be private, not government based, and could be spread across multiple organizations in Mexico and elsewhere. However, to develop a core research capacity that addresses the most important policy questions related to police reform and corruption, there should be some form of government funding, though it could also be supplemented with private support. Furthermore, funding should depend on a blind assessment of the quality of research proposals by different organizations, to help ensure that the research is not itself influenced by corruption. The research capability should address both short-term policy issues and long-term issues of enduring concern. The research should be based on sound technical standards, subject to peer review, disseminated publicly, cost-effective, and timely.

It is instructive to note that development of data and analysis capability was part of the transition the United States made from a conscripted to an all-volunteer military force. When the draft was eliminated in 1973, the U.S. Congress simultaneously authorized the creation of the Defense Manpower Data Center to collect, clean, and maintain administrative and survey data related to military manpower and personnel in the United States. Furthermore, Congress authorized funding for research centers devoted to providing research to support military personnel policies. These organizations included the Military Manpower Research Center at RAND (the original name of the research center at RAND focusing on military manpower), the U.S. Army Research Institute, the Center for Naval Analyses, and the RAND Arroyo Center. These capabilities took time to grow, but they provide important policy analyses, such as those summarized in Chapter Two. Though the capabilities required to collect and analyze data related to police reform and corruption in Mexico would need to be developed for Mexico's specific context, the experience of the U.S. military shows that such an endeavor can be developed successfully.

A proposal to create an agency in Mexico that would develop and track security-related indicators has been on the table since the 2008 National Agreement for Security, Justice and Legality (see Sabet, 2010a) signed into law by representatives of each branch of government and by state governments and members of civil society (e.g., unions and religious groups). The proposal sought to increase professionalism of law enforcement in Mexico and included provisions that would involve greater information sharing among government agencies regarding security matters. The proposal also called for a system of citizen oversight of police that would allow citizens to inform on suspected criminals and make complaints against officers. Such an agreement is an important first step toward developing a national oversight agency. However, full implementation will require develop and maintenance of data systems that cover a range of areas, including police personnel information and information on compensation and personnel policies.

Specific Research Areas

A step toward developing a data and research capability is identifying a set of research questions and policy issues that can guide a research agenda. These questions and issues could be pursued in the short term with ad hoc data collection efforts, such as surveys, and benefit from long-term projects as Mexico's data capability is further developed. This subsection identifies specific, data-driven research questions related to police reform and corruption in Mexico.

Effectiveness of Municipal Police Reform Efforts: The Commission on Accreditation for Law Enforcement Agencies and the Subsidy for Municipal Public Security. A key goal for future empirical research should be to assess police reform program effectiveness. Specifically, future work should determine whether current reforms are effective and, if so, to what degree and based on what outcomes. For example, some municipal police forces in Mexico have adopted the CALEA accreditation model. CALEA is a U.S.-based organization, created in 1979, to improve the delivery of public safety services by providing a set of standards, establishing and administering an accreditation process, and recognizing those who achieve the standards. A key question is whether adoption of CALEA in Mexico has improved law enforcement outcomes and reduced police corruption.

A program evaluation of CALEA could be conducted by taking advantage of the fact that the program has not been uniformly adopted throughout Mexico. Using an analytic approach, known as difference in differences, one could compare the outcomes of municipalities that have adopted CALEA with those of municipalities with similar characteristics that have not, and compare both sets of municipalities before and after CALEA was adopted. Therefore, the data would have to cover the period before and after CALEA adoption in both municipalities that adopted CALEA and those that did not. If there is information on those that plan to adopt CALEA in the future, one could conduct surveys before and after and in both types of locations. If there is no advance knowledge of CALEA adoption, this type of analysis would have to rely on existing data on crime, corruption perceptions, and demographic characteristics of households in each type of municipality, as a first step. That is, one can rely on existing data sources, supplemented with data collected by survey. Such an analysis would provide an estimate of whether CALEA improves law enforcement outcomes in Mexico and by how much.

Similarly, as described in Chapter Three, SUBSEMUN is a federal initiative targeted at municipal public security and provides federal funds that supplement local efforts to professionalize and modernize municipal police forces. The funds must be used in targeted ways, and a key question is how effective this approach is in improving police force quality and management—and specifically corruption. Because municipalities with the highest crime rates are more likely to receive these funds, the program is not randomly assigned to different municipalities. An assessment of this program would have to explicitly account for this selection effect for program inclusion and, like the CALEA program, could rely on existing data sources as a first step, followed by a data collection effort that includes qualitative interviews of those knowledgeable about the program and in various municipalities.

The Effects That Political Disruption Can Have on Police Corruption. Sabet (2010a, 2010b) argues that the lack of political continuity and the constant turnover of politicians, driven by term limits, means that reforms are disrupted at best, or short-lived at worst. Ferraz and Finan (2008) find that municipalities in Brazil where mayors get reelected experience significantly less corruption than municipalities where they are not. Thus, political disruption could be fueling police corruption in Mexico.

This research topic would use empirical data to rigorously assess whether political turnover fuels police corruption in Mexico. Such an analysis would require a sample of municipalities, matched on key characteristics, with variations in political turnover. Levitt (1997) finds that the size of the police force increases substantially in mayoral and gubernatorial election years. A similar approach could be used to assess crime and corruption perceptions data based on the timing of elections at the municipal level. Data could be obtained through a survey of municipal police forces.

Surveying the Police in Mexico: Toward Understanding the Characteristics and Career Paths of Police in Mexico and Their Perceptions About Reform. This research effort would involve conducting a survey of police in Mexico to understand qualifications, pay, promotions, separation decisions, duty assignments, demographic characteristics, and police perceptions of anticorruption reforms. The survey would be a large random sample of police at each level (municipal, state, and federal) and would focus on obtaining basic background information, information on past and current corruption, and the status of current reforms. Not only would this type of survey provide a detailed assessment of key issues related to police forces in Mexico; it could also be used as a baseline to assess future reform efforts.

Corruption of the Armed Services in Mexico. Although corruption perceptions data show that the Mexican public has greater confidence in the armed forces than in the police forces when it comes to corruption, concern still remains about corruption among those in the armed services in Mexico. For example, the Justice in Mexico Project's March 2010 report states that 40 members of the armed forces are serving prison time for having links to drug-trafficking organizations. Such concerns have led some policymakers in Mexico to consider transferring responsibilities related to combating the drug trade that currently reside with the military back to the state and local law enforcement agencies (Justice in Mexico Project, 2010a).

Little information is available about corruption in the armed services in Mexico or the factors that have led to the perception that corruption is generally less in the armed services than in the police forces. Why are the armed services perceived as less corrupt? Is this based on fact? If so, what factors lead to a military force that is less corrupt than the police force? A survey of armed forces personnel coupled with access to administrative data on these personnel could be used to address these questions.

Understanding the Effects That Eligibility Screening and Police Firings Can Have on Corruption. Applicants and current law enforcement officers are screened to ensure that they meet a range of eligibility criteria for employment. Such screening was introduced to increase the professionalism of the Mexican security forces. However, recent news articles suggest that large numbers of Mexican police have been fired for failing to meet these criteria, especially polygraphs and other exams designed to test their trustworthiness. Others are fired for violating various rules; for example, about 15 percent of municipal police in Monterrey were fired in the first half of 2010 for rule violations.

A key question is whether these measures actually improve the professionalism of the Mexican police forces. Although removing violators or those who are deemed untrustworthy would seem to eliminate problems, these violators are replaced by new hires who then operate in the same environment as those who are fired or screened out. On the other hand, such firings can send a powerful message to others that poor behavior is not tolerated, improving the professionalism of those retained. In short, data are needed to sort out the effectiveness of this strategy of increasing professionalism.

This research effort would involve conducting a survey of police using a choice-based sampling methodology in municipalities that have been matched on the characteristics of the communities they serve and on police human resource policies, particularly screening and firing policies. Interviews of police administrators can also be conducted, and access to administrative data, if available, can be used to assess how screening and firing affect outcomes related to corruption and professionalism.

Conclusions

The purpose of this report is to provide information on some of the roots of police corruption in Mexico and on compensation and personnel policies that can help mitigate corruption. We analyzed household and corruption data to provide an initial assessment of the effectiveness of recent police reforms in Mexico. Although the study provides indications of progress with respect to professionalizing the police forces in Mexico and reducing the relative growth of police corruption, it is clear that more needs to be done. We drew from available data sources to understand the current situation with respect to the professionalization of the Mexican police and to corruption, but, in general, the available data are inadequate to do all but the most basic and cursory assessment of effectiveness of recent reforms. To better inform policy-setting and improve accountability and transparency, better data and more sophisticated analytical methods are required. Part of future reforms to combat police corruption in Mexico should include a plan for the collection and analysis of data on police.

Bibliography

Acemoglu, Daron, Simon Johnson, and James A. Robinson, "Institutions as a Fundamental Cause of Long-Run Growth," in Philippe Aghion and Steven Durlauf, eds., *Handbook of Economic Growth*, Volume IA, Amsterdam: Elsevier, 2005, pp. 385–472.

Ades, Alberto, and Rafael Di Tella, "Rents, Competition, and Corruption," *American Economic Review*, Vol. 89, No. 4, September 1999, pp. 982–993.

Aidt, Toke, "Economic Analysis of Corruption: A Survey," *Economic Journal*, Vol. 113, No. 491, November 2003, pp. F632–F652.

Altonji, Joseph G., and Rebecca M. Blank, "Race and Gender in the Labor Market," *Handbook of Labor Economics*, Vol. 3, Part 3, 1999, pp. 3143–3259.

Andvig, Jens Christopher, and Odd-Helge Fjeldstad, *Corruption: A Review of Contemporary Research*, with Inge Amundsen, Tone Sissener, and Tina Søreide, Bergen, Norway: Chr. Michelsen Institute, Development Studies and Human Rights, R 2001:7, 2001.

Arndt, Christiane, and Charles Oman, *Uses and Abuses of Governance Indicators*, Paris: Development Centre of the Organisation for Economic Co-Operation and Development, 2006.

Asch, Beth J., "The Economic Complexities of Incentive Reforms," in Robert Klitgaard and Paul C. Light, eds., *High-Performance Government: Structure, Leadership, Incentives*, Santa Monica, Calif.: RAND Corporation, MG-256-PRGS, 2005, pp. 309–343. As of June 10, 2011:
http://www.rand.org/pubs/monographs/MG256.html

Asch, Beth J., and Paul Heaton, *An Analysis of the Incidence of Recruiter Irregularities*, Santa Monica, Calif.: RAND Corporation, TR-827-OSD, 2010. As of June 10, 2011:
http://www.rand.org/pubs/technical_reports/TR827.html

Asch, Beth J., Paul Heaton, James Hosek, Francisco Martorell, Curtis Simon, and John T. Warner, *Cash Incentives and Military Enlistment, Attrition, and Reenlistment*, Santa Monica, Calif.: RAND Corporation, MG-950-OSD, 2010. As of April 18, 2011:
http://www.rand.org/pubs/monographs/MG950.html

Asch, Beth J., and James Hosek, *Military Compensation: Trends and Policy Options*, Santa Monica, Calif.: RAND Corporation, DB-273-OSD, 1999. As of April 18, 2011:
http://www.rand.org/pubs/documented_briefings/DB273.html

Asch, Beth J., and John T. Warner, *A Policy Analysis of Alternative Military Retirement Systems*, Santa Monica, Calif.: RAND Corporation, MR-465-OSD, 1994. As of June 10, 2011:
http://www.rand.org/pubs/monograph_reports/MR465.html

———, "A Theory of Compensation and Personnel Policy in Hierarchical Organizations with Application to the United States Military," *Journal of Labor Economics*, Vol. 19, No. 3, July 2001, pp. 523–562.

Azfar, Omar, and William Robert Nelson, "Transparency, Wages, and the Separation of Powers: An Experimental Analysis of Corruption," *Public Choice*, Vol. 130, No. 3–4, March 2007, pp. 471–493.

Bardhan, Pranab, and Dilip Mookherjee, "Decentralisation and Accountability in Infrastructure Delivery in Developing Countries," *Economic Journal*, Vol. 116, No. 508, January 2006, pp. 101–127.

Barr, Abigail, Magnus Lindelow, and Pieter Serneels, *To Serve the Community or Oneself: The Public Servant's Dilemma*, World Bank, Policy Research Working Paper WPS3187, January 15, 2004. As of April 18, 2011: http://go.worldbank.org/QOMHXY3JG0

Becker, Gary S., and George J. Stigler, "Law Enforcement, Malfeasance, and Compensation of Enforcers," *Journal of Legal Studies*, Vol. 3, No. 1, January 1974, pp. 1–18.

Birns, Larry, and Alex Sánchez, "The Government and the Drug Lords: Who Rules Mexico?" Council on Hemispheric Affairs, April 1, 2007. As of April 18, 2011: http://www.coha.org/the-government-and-the-druglords-who-rules-mexico/

Borjas, George J., *The Wage Structure and the Sorting of Workers into the Public Sector*, Cambridge, Mass.: National Bureau of Economic Research, working paper 9313, October 2002. As of April 18, 2011: http://www.nber.org/papers/w9313

Brunetti, Aymo, and Beatrice Weder, "A Free Press Is Bad News for Corruption," *Journal of Public Economics*, Vol. 89, No. 7–8, August 2003, pp. 1801–1824.

Buddin, Richard, *Success of First-Term Soldiers: The Effects of Recruiting Practices and Recruit Characteristics*, Santa Monica, Calif.: RAND Corporation, MG-262-A, 2005. As of April 18, 2011: http://www.rand.org/pubs/monographs/MG262.html

Burgess, Simon, and Marisa Ratto, "The Role of Incentives in the Public Sector: Issues and Evidence," *Oxford Review of Economic Policy*, Vol. 19, No. 2, 2003, pp. 285–300.

Chabat, Jorge, "Mexico: The Security Challenge," in Jordi Díez, ed., *Canadian and Mexican Security in the New North America: Challenges and Prospects*, Montréal: McGill-Queen's University Press, 2006, pp. 51–69.

DellaVigna, Stefano, and Eliana La Ferrara, "Detecting Illegal Arms Trade," *American Economic Journal: Economic Policy*, Vol. 2, No. 4, November 2010, pp. 26–57.

Demougin, Dominique, and Claude Fluet, "Monitoring Versus Incentives," *European Economic Review*, Vol. 45, No. 9, October 2001, pp. 1741–1764.

Dewatripont, Mathias, Ian Jewitt, and Jean Tirole, "The Economics of Career Concerns, Part II: Application to Missions and Accountability of Government Agencies," *Review of Economic Studies*, Vol. 66, No. 1, January 1999, pp. 199–217.

Di Tella, Rafael, and Ernesto Schargrodsky, "The Role of Wages and Auditing During a Crackdown on Corruption in the City of Buenos Aires," *Journal of Law and Economics*, Vol. 46, No. 1, April 2003, pp. 269–92.

Dixit, Avinash, "Incentives and Organizations in the Public Sector: An Interpretative Review," *Journal of Human Resources*, Vol. 37, No. 4, Autumn 2002, pp. 696–727.

Djankov, Simeon, Edward Glaeser, Rafael La Porta, Florencio Lopez-de-Silanes, and Andrei Shleifer, "The New Comparative Economics," *Journal of Comparative Economics*, Vol. 31, No. 4, December 2003, pp. 595–619.

Djankov, Simeon, Rafael La Porta, Florencio Lopez-de-Silanes, and Andrei Shleifer, "Disclosure by Politicians," *American Economic Journal: Applied Economics*, Vol. 2, No. 2, April 2010, pp. 179–209.

Egel, Daniel, "Tribal Diversity, Political Patronage and the Yemeni Decentralization Experiment," working paper, November 19, 2009. As of October 19, 2010: http://www.egels.org/daniel/Research_files/Egel_Tribes.pdf

Ellingwood, Ken, "Fixing Mexico Police Becomes a Priority," *Los Angeles Times*, November 17, 2009. As of October 19, 2010: http://www.latimes.com/news/nationworld/world/la-fg-mexico-police17-2009nov17,0,2236458.story

———, "Mexico Fires 3,200 Federal Police Officers," *Los Angeles Times*, August 31, 2010. As of October 19, 2010: http://articles.latimes.com/2010/aug/31/world/la-fg-mexico-police-fired-20100831

Embassy of the United States, Mexico City, Mexico, "Merida Initiative at a Glance: Combating Violence in Juárez, September 2010.

Estados Unidos Mexicanos, *Diario Oficial de la Federacion*, 2008. As of June 21, 2011:
http://www.dof.gob.mx/nota_to_imagen_fs.php?cod_diario=213097&pagina=1&seccion=1

Fama, Eugene F., "Agency Problems and the Theory of the Firm," *Journal of Political Economy*, Vol. 88, No. 2, April 1980, pp. 288–307.

Ferraz, Claudio, and Federico Finan, *Motivating Politicians: The Impacts of Monetary Incentives on Quality and Performance*, Bonn: Institute for the Study of Labor, discussion paper 3411, March 2008.

Fisman, Raymond, and Roberta Gatti, "Decentralization and Corruption: Evidence Across Countries," *Journal of Public Economics*, Vol. 83, No. 3, March 2002, pp. 325–345.

Flakus, Greg, "Drug Money Worsens Corruption in Mexico," *Voice of America News*, March 25, 2008. As of October 20, 2010:
http://www.voanews.com/khmer-english/news/a-40-2008-03-25-voa5-90166507.html

Gerring, John, and Strom C. Thacker, "Political Institutions and Corruption: The Role of Unitarism and Parliamentarism," *British Journal of Political Science*, Vol. 34, No. 2, 2004, pp. 295–330.

Gibbons, Robert, and Kevin J. Murphy, "Optimal Incentive Contracts in the Presence of Career Concerns: Theory and Evidence," *Journal of Political Economy*, Vol. 100, No. 3, June 1992, pp. 468–505.

Gibbs, Michael, *Pay Competitiveness and Quality of Department of Defense Scientists and Engineers*, Santa Monica, Calif.: RAND Corporation, MR-1312-OSD, 2001. As of April 18, 2011:
http://www.rand.org/pubs/monograph_reports/MR1312.html

Goldberg, Matthew S., *A Survey of Enlisted Retention: Models and Findings*, Alexandria, Va.: Center for Naval Analyses, D0004085.A2, 2001. As of April 18, 2011:
http://www.cna.org/research/2001/survey-enlisted-retention-models-findings

Gorodnichenko, Yuriy, and Klara Sabirianova Peter, "Public Sector Pay and Corruption: Measuring Bribery from Micro Data," *Journal of Public Economics*, Vol. 91, No. 5–6, June 2007, pp. 963–991.

Guasch, J. Luis, and Andrew Weiss, "Self-Selection in the Labor Market," *American Economic Review*, Vol. 71, No. 3, June 1981, pp. 275–284.

Hansen, Michael L., and Jennie W. Wenger, *Why Do Pay Elasticity Estimates Differ?* Alexandria, Va.: Center for Naval Analyses, D0005644.A2, November 2002. As of April 18, 2011:
http://handle.dtic.mil/100.2/ADA407366

Harrell, Margaret C., and William M. Hix, *Managing Adverse and Reportable Information Regarding General and Flag Officers*, Santa Monica, Calif.: RAND Corporation, forthcoming.

Hogan, Paul F., Javier Espinosa, Patrick Mackin, and Peter Greenston, *A Model of Army Reenlistment Behavior: Estimates of the Effects of Army's Selective Reenlistment Bonus on Retention by Occupation*, Arlington, Va.: U.S. Army Research Institute for the Behavioral and Social Sciences, June 2005.

Holmstrom, Bengt, "Managerial Incentive Schemes: A Dynamic Perspective," in *Essays in Economics and Management in Honour of Lars Wahlbeck*, Helsingfors: Svenska Handelshögskolan, 1982, pp. 169–182.

Holmstrom, Bengt, and Paul Milgrom, "Multitask Principal–Agent Analyses: Incentive Contracts, Asset Ownership, and Job Design," *Journal of Law, Economics, and Organization*, Vol. 7 (special issue), 1991, pp. 24–52.

Hosek, James, and Paco Martorell, *How Have Deployments During the War on Terrorism Affected Reenlistment?* Santa Monica, Calif.: RAND Corporation, MG-873-OSD, 2009. As of June 9, 2011:
http://www.rand.org/pubs/monographs/MG873.html

Hosek, James R., John T. Warner, and Beth J. Asch, "New Economics of Manpower in the Post–Cold War Era," in Todd Sandler and Keith Hartley, eds., *Handbook of Defense Economics*, Volume 2: *Defense in a Globalized World*, Amsterdam: Elsevier North Holland, 2007, pp. 1075–1138.

Hsieh, Chang-Tai, and Enrico Moretti, "Did Iraq Cheat the United Nations? Underpricing, Bribes, and the Oil for Food Program," *Quarterly Journal of Economics*, Vol. 121, No. 4, 2006, pp. 1211–1248.

Ichniowski, Casey, Kathryn Shaw, and Giovanna Prennushi, "The Effects of Human Resource Management Practices on Productivity: A Study of Steel Finishing Lines," *American Economic Review*, Vol. 87, No. 3, June 1997, pp. 291–313.

Instituto Ciudadano de Estudios Sobre la Inseguridad, *Encuesta Nacional Sobre Inseguridad* [National Survey on Insecurity], ENSI-3, 2005. As of April 18, 2011:
http://www.icesi.org.mx/estadisticas/estadisticas_encuestasNacionales_ensi3.asp

———, *Encuesta Nacional Sobre Inseguridad* [National Survey on Insecurity], ENSI-5, 2008. As of April 18, 2011:
http://www.icesi.org.mx/estadisticas/estadisticas_encuestasNacionales_ensi5b.asp

———, *Encuesta Nacional Sobre Inseguridad* [National Survey on Insecurity], ENSI-6, 2009. As of April 18, 2011:
http://www.icesi.org.mx/estadisticas/estadisticas_encuestasNacionales_ensi6.asp

Instituto Nacional de Estadística y Geografía, *Encuesta Nacional de Ingreso y Gasto de los Hogares* [National Survey of Household Income and Expenditure], 2000. As of April 18, 2011:
http://www.inegi.org.mx/est/contenidos/Proyectos/Encuestas/Hogares/regulares/Enigh/Enigh2000/default.aspx

———, *Encuesta Nacional de Ingreso y Gasto de los Hogares* [National Survey of Household Income and Expenditure], 2002. As of April 18, 2011:
http://www.inegi.org.mx/est/contenidos/Proyectos/Encuestas/Hogares/regulares/Enigh/Enigh2002/default.aspx

———, *Encuesta Nacional de Ingreso y Gasto de los Hogares* [National Survey of Household Income and Expenditure], 2004. As of April 18, 2011:
http://www.inegi.org.mx/est/contenidos/Proyectos/Encuestas/Hogares/regulares/Enigh/Enigh2004/default.aspx

———, *Encuesta Nacional de Ingreso y Gasto de los Hogares* [National Survey of Household Income and Expenditure], 2005. As of April 18, 2011:
http://www.inegi.org.mx/est/contenidos/Proyectos/Encuestas/Hogares/regulares/Enigh/Enigh2005/default.aspx

———, *Encuesta Nacional de Ingreso y Gasto de los Hogares* [National Survey of Household Income and Expenditure], 2006. As of April 18, 2011:
http://www.inegi.org.mx/est/contenidos/Proyectos/Encuestas/Hogares/regulares/Enigh/Enigh2006/default.aspx

———, *Encuesta Nacional de Ingreso y Gasto de los Hogares* [National Survey of Household Income and Expenditure], 2008. As of April 18, 2011:
http://www.inegi.org.mx/est/contenidos/Proyectos/Encuestas/Hogares/regulares/Enigh/Enigh2008/tradicional/default.aspx

Jacob, Brian A., and Steven D. Levitt, "Rotten Apples: An Investigation of the Prevalence and Predictors of Teacher Cheating," *Quarterly Journal of Economics*, Vol. 118, No. 3, August 2003, pp. 843–877.

Jacquemet, Nicolas, *Corruption as Betrayal: Experimental Evidence on Corruption Under Delegation*, University of Lyons II and Laval University, 2005. As of April 18, 2011:
http://halshs.archives-ouvertes.fr/halshs-00180044/en/

June, Raymond, Afroza Chowdhury, Nathaniel Heller, and Jonathan Werve, *A Users' Guide to Measuring Corruption*, Oslo: UNDP Oslo Governance Center, 2008.

Justice in Mexico Project, *Justice in Mexico News Report*, March 2009a. As of April 20, 2011:
http://catcher.sandiego.edu/items/peacestudies/march2009.pdf

———, *Justice in Mexico News Report*, June 2009b. As of April 20, 2011:
http://catcher.sandiego.edu/items/peacestudies/JMPjune2009.pdf

———, *Justice in Mexico News Report*, March 2010a. As of April 21, 2011:
http://catcher.sandiego.edu/items/peacestudies/march2010.pdf

————, *Justice in Mexico News Report*, May 2010b. As of April 20, 2011:
http://catcher.sandiego.edu/items/peacestudies/may2010.pdf

————, *Justice in Mexico News Report*, June 2010c. As of April 20, 2011:
http://catcher.sandiego.edu/items/peacestudies/june2010.pdf

Katz, Lawrence F., and Alan B. Krueger, *Changes in the Structure of Wages in the Public and Private Sectors*, Cambridge, Mass.: National Bureau of Economic Research, working paper 3667, March 1991. As of April 18, 2011:
http://www.nber.org/papers/w3667

Khwaja, Asim Ijaz, and Atif Mian, "Do Lenders Favor Politically Connected Firms? Rent Provision in an Emerging Financial Market," *Quarterly Journal of Economics*, Vol. 120, No. 4, November 2005, pp. 1371–1411.

Klerman, Jacob Alex, and Arleen Leibowitz, "Job Continuity Among New Mothers," *Demography*, Vol. 36, No. 2, May 1999, pp. 145–155. As of June 14, 2011:
http://www.rand.org/pubs/reprints/RP804.html

Knack, Stephen, "Measuring Corruption: A Critique of Indicators in Eastern Europe and Central Asia," *Journal of Public Policy*, Vol. 27, No. 3, 2007, pp. 255–291.

LaRose, Anthony P., and Sean A. Maddan, "Reforming La Policía: Looking to the Future of Policing in Mexico," *Police Practice and Research: An International Journal*, Vol. 10, No. 4, 2009, pp. 333–348.

Lazear, Edward P., "Why Is There Mandatory Retirement?" *Journal of Political Economy*, Vol. 87, No. 6, December 1979, pp. 1261–1264.

————, "Pensions as Severance Pay," in Zvi Bodie and John B. Shoven, eds., *Financial Aspects of the United States Pension System*, Chicago, Ill.: University of Chicago Press, 1983, pp. 57–89.

————, "Salaries and Piece Rates," *Journal of Business*, Vol. 59, No. 3, July 1986, pp. 405–431.

————, *Personnel Economics*, Cambridge, Mass.: MIT Press, 1995.

Lazear, Edward P., and Michael Gibbs, *Personnel Economics in Practice*, 2nd ed., Hoboken, N.J.: John Wiley and Sons, 2009.

Lazear, Edward P., and Sherwin Rosen, "Rank-Order Tournaments as Optimum Labor Contracts," *Journal of Political Economy*, Vol. 89, No. 5, October 1981, pp. 841–864.

Lecuona, Guillermo Zapeda, "Mexican Police and the Criminal Justice System," in Robert A. Donnelly and David A. Shirk, eds., *Police and Public Security in Mexico*, San Diego, Calif.: University Readers, 2009, pp. 39–64.

Lederman, Daniel, Norman V. Loayza, and Rodrigo R. Soares, "Accountability and Corruption: Political Institutions Matter," *Economics and Politics*, Vol. 17, No. 1, March 2005, pp. 1–35.

Levitt, Steven D., "Using Electoral Cycles in Police Hiring to Estimate the Effect of Police on Crime," *American Economic Review*, Vol. 87, No. 3, June 1997, pp. 270–290.

Lyons, John, "Mexico's Cops Seek Upgrade," *Wall Street Journal*, October 24, 2009. As of October 20, 2010:
http://online.wsj.com/article/SB125251965257196475.html

"Mapa interactivo: Policía Única," *El Universal*, October 18, 2010. As of April 18, 2011:
http://www.eluniversal.com.mx/notas/716994.html

Mayberry, Paul W., and Neil B. Carey, "The Effects of Aptitude and Experience on Mechanical Job Performance," *Educational and Psychological Measurement*, Vol. 57, No. 1, February 1997, pp. 131–149.

McMillan, John, and Pablo Zoido, "How to Subvert Democracy: Montesinos in Peru," *Journal of Economic Perspectives*, Vol. 18, No. 4, Autumn 2004, pp. 69–92.

Meyer, Maureen, "At a Crossroads: Drug Trafficking, Violence and the Mexican State," Washington Office on Latin America, Beckley Foundation Drug Policy Programme, briefing paper 13, November 2007.

Mohar, Edgar, former Secretary of Citizen Security, Querétaro, "Twenty Years of Police Reform in Querétaro: What's Working and What's Not?" presentation at Police Reform in Mexico: Challenges and Opportunities to Strengthen Law Enforcement at the State and Local Level, Woodrow Wilson International Center for Scholars, Mexico Institute, September 17, 2009. As of April 18, 2011:
http://www.wilsoncenter.org/events/docs/Edgar_Mohar.ppt

Moloeznik, Marcos Pablo, "The Militarization of Public Security in Mexico," in Robert Donnelly and David Shirk, eds., *Police and Public Security in Mexico*, San Diego, Calif.: University Readers, 2009, pp. 65–92.

Moore, Carole, Paul Hogan, Christian Kirchner, Patrick C. Mackin, and Peter M. Greenston, *Econometric Estimates of Army Retention: Zones A, B, C, D and Retirement-Eligible, 1990–2004*, Arlington, Va.: U.S. Army Research Institute for the Behavioral and Social Sciences, 2007. As of April 18, 2011:
http://www.dtic.mil/cgi-bin/GetTRDoc?AD=ADA464636&Location=U2&doc=GetTRDoc.pdf

Morris, Stephen D., "Corruption and the Mexican Political System: Continuity and Change," *Third World Quarterly*, Vol. 20, No. 3, 1999, pp. 623–643.

———, "Political Corruption in Mexico: An Empirical Analysis," working paper, 2003. As of October 20, 2010:
http://blueweb.mtsu.edu/politicalscience/faculty/documents/crptn_in_Mexico_lasa2003.pdf

———, "Corruption and Change in Mexico," draft manuscript presented at the 54th annual meeting of the South Eastern Council of Latin American Studies, San Jose, Costa Rica, April 2007.

———, "Mexico: Corruption and Change," in Stephen D. Morris and Charles H. Blake, eds., *Corruption and Politics in Latin America: National and Regional Dynamics*, Boulder, Colo.: Lynne Rienner Publishers, 2010, pp. 137–164.

National Defense Research Institute, *Sexual Orientation and U.S. Military Personnel Policy: An Update of RAND's 1993 Study*, Santa Monica, Calif.: RAND Corporation, MG-1056-OSD, 2010. As of June 10, 2011:
http://www.rand.org/pubs/monographs/MG1056.html

Olken, Benjamin A., "Corruption and the Costs of Redistribution: Micro Evidence from Indonesia," *Journal of Public Economics*, Vol. 90, No. 4–5, May 2006, pp. 853–870.

———, "Monitoring Corruption: Evidence from a Field Experiment in Indonesia," *Journal of Political Economy*, Vol. 115, No. 2, April 2007, pp. 200–249.

———, "Corruption Perceptions vs. Corruption Reality," *Journal of Public Economics*, Vol. 93, No. 7–8, August 2009, pp. 950–964.

Olson, Alexandra, "Mexico Fired 10 Percent of Federal Police in 2010," *Washington Times*, August 30, 2010. As of October 20, 2010:
http://www.washingtontimes.com/news/2010/aug/30/mexico-fired-10-percent-federal-police-2010/

Olson, Eric L., "Police Reform and Modernization in Mexico, 2009," Woodrow Wilson International Center for Scholars, Mexico Institute, policy brief, September 2009. As of April 18, 2011:
http://www.wilsoncenter.org/news/docs/Brief%20on%20Police%20Reform%20and%20Modernization.pdf

Ostrom, Elinor, "An Agenda for the Study of Institutions," *Public Choice*, Vol. 48, No. 1, 1986, pp. 3–25.

Palmier, Leslie H., *The Control of Bureaucratic Corruption: Case Studies in Asia*, New Delhi: Allied Publishers, 1985.

Polich, J. Michael, James N. Dertouzos, and S. James Press, *The Enlistment Bonus Experiment*, Santa Monica, Calif.: RAND Corporation, R-3353-FMP, 1986. As of April 18, 2011:
http://www.rand.org/pubs/reports/R3353.html

Prendergast, Canice, "The Provision of Incentives in Firms," *Journal of Economic Literature*, Vol. 37, No. 1, March 1999, pp. 7–63.

———, *Selection and Oversight in the Public Sector, with the Los Angeles Police Department as an Example*, Cambridge, Mass.: National Bureau of Economic Research, working paper 8664, December 2001. As of April 18, 2011:
http://www.nber.org/papers/w8664

Project A: The U.S. Army Selection and Classification Project (Special Issue), *Personnel Psychology*, Vol. 43, No. 2, 1990.

Quah, Jon S. T., "Corruption in Asian Countries: Can It Be Minimized?" *Public Administration Review*, Vol. 59, No. 6, November–December 1999, pp. 483–494.

————, "Combating Corruption in Singapore: What Can Be Learned?" *Journal of Contingencies and Crisis Management*, Vol. 9, No. 1, March 2001, pp. 29–35.

Reames, Benjamin, "Police Forces in Mexico: A Profile," paper presented at Reforming the Administration of Justice in Mexico conference, Center for U.S. Mexican Studies, May 2003.

Reinikka, Ritva, and Jakob Svensson, "Local Capture: Evidence from a Central Government Transfer Program in Uganda," *Quarterly Journal of Economics*, Vol. 119, No. 2, May 2004, pp. 678–704.

————, "Fighting Corruption to Improve Schooling: Evidence from a Newspaper Campaign in Uganda," *Journal of the European Economic Association*, Vol. 3, No. 2–3, April–May 2005, pp. 259–267.

Rosen, Sherwin, "Authority, Control, and the Distribution of Earnings," *Bell Journal of Economics*, Vol. 13, No. 2, Autumn 1982, pp. 311–323.

Sabet, Daniel, "Troubled Reforms: Efforts to Professionalize Local Law Enforcement in Mexico," working paper, February 2009. As of April 19, 2011:
http://www9.georgetown.edu/faculty/dms76/Policefiles/Police_Frame.htm

————, *Police Reform in Mexico: Advances and Persistent Obstacles*, Woodrow Wilson International Center for Scholars, Mexico Institute, University of San Diego Trans-Border Institute, Working Paper Series on U.S.-Mexico Security Collaboration, May 2010a. As of April 19, 2011:
http://www9.georgetown.edu/faculty/dms76/Policefiles/Sabet_police_reform.pdf

————, "Corruption vs. Professionalism: The Challenge of Police Reform in Mexico," draft manuscript, Georgetown University, November 2010b.

Salgado, Juan, Center for Economic Research and Education, Mexico City, "Needs Assessment for Bottom-Up Police Reform in Mexico," unpublished presentation to the Woodrow Wilson International Center for Scholars conference on Police Reform in Mexico, Washington, D.C., September 2009.

Schaefer, Agnes Gereben, Benjamin Bahney, and K. Jack Riley, *Security in Mexico: Implications for U.S. Policy Options*, Santa Monica, Calif.: RAND Corporation, MG-876-RC, 2009. As of April 19, 2011:
http://www.rand.org/pubs/monographs/MG876.html

Secretaría de Seguridad Pública, *Sistema Integral de Desarrollo Policial*, Mexico City, 2009.

Sellman, W. Steven, "Public Policy Implications for Military Entrance Standards," keynote address presented at the 39th Annual Conference of the International Military Testing Association, Sydney, Australia, October 14–16, 1997.

Shelley, Louise, "Corruption and Organized Crime in Mexico in the Post-PRI Transition," *Journal of Contemporary Criminal Justice*, Vol. 17, No. 3, August 2001, pp. 213–231.

Shi, Lan, "The Limit of Oversight in Policing: Evidence from the 2001 Cincinnati Riot," *Journal of Public Economics*, Vol. 93, No. 1–2, February 2009, pp. 99–113.

Shleifer, Andrei, and Robert W. Vishny, "Corruption," *Quarterly Journal of Economics*, Vol. 108, No. 3, August 1993, pp. 599–617.

Siddiquee, Noore Alam, "Combating Corruption and Managing Integrity in Malaysia: A Critical Overview of Recent Strategies and Initiatives," *Public Organization Review*, Vol. 10, No. 2, June 2010, pp. 153–171.

Simon, Curtis J. and John T. Warner, "Managing the All-Volunteer Force in a Time of War," *Economics of Peace and Security Journal*, Vol. 2, No. 1, January 2007, pp. 20–29.

Svensson, Jakob, "Eight Questions About Corruption," *Journal of Economic Perspectives*, Vol. 19, No. 3, Summer 2005, pp. 19–42.

TI—*See* Transparency International.

Tirole, Jean, "The Internal Organization of Government," *Oxford Economic Papers*, Vol. 46, No. 1, 1994, pp. 1–29.

Transparencia Mexicana, *Encuesta Nacional de Corrupción y Buen Gobierno* [National Survey of Corruption and Good Government], 2001.

———, *Encuesta Nacional de Corrupción y Buen Gobierno* [National Survey of Corruption and Good Government], 2003.

———, *Encuesta Nacional de Corrupción y Buen Gobierno* [National Survey of Corruption and Good Government], 2005.

———, *Encuesta Nacional de Corrupción y Buen Gobierno* [National Survey of Corruption and Good Government], 2007.

Transparency International, "Corruption Perceptions Index 2009," c. 2009. As of October 20, 2010: http://www.transparency.org/policy_research/surveys_indices/cpi/2009

Treisman, Daniel, "The Causes of Corruption: A Cross-National Study," *Journal of Public Economics*, Vol. 76, No. 3, June 2000, pp. 399–457.

———, "Decentralization and the Quality of Government," working paper, October 2002. As of October 20, 2010: http://www.sscnet.ucla.edu/polisci/faculty/treisman/Papers/DecandGovt.pdf

Van Rijckeghem, Caroline, and Beatrice Weder, "Bureaucratic Corruption and the Rate of Temptation: Do Wages in the Civil Service Affect Corruption, and by How Much?" *Journal of Development Economics*, Vol. 65, No. 2, August 2001, pp. 307–331.

Warner, John T., and Beth J. Asch, "The Economics of Military Manpower," in Keith Hartley and Todd Sandler, eds., *Handbook of Defense Economics*, Volume 1, Amsterdam: Elsevier, 1995, pp. 347–398.

Weiss, Andrew W., "Job Queues and Layoffs in Labor Markets with Flexible Wages," *Journal of Political Economy*, Vol. 88, No. 3, June 1980, pp. 526–538.

Wilson, James Q., *Bureaucracy: What Government Agencies Do and Why They Do It*, New York: Basic Books, 1989.

Woodruff, Christopher, "Measuring Institutions," in Susan Rose-Ackerman, ed., *International Handbook of the Economics of Corruption*, Northampton, Mass.: Edward Elgar, 2006, pp. 105–126.